REST IN GREEN PASTURES

REST
IN GREEN PASTURES

ENCOURAGEMENT FOR SHEPHERDS

Edited by Chris McCurley

© 2015 by Start2Finish

All rights reserved. No part of this publication may be reproduced, stored in a retrieval system, or transmitted in any form or by any means without the prior written permission of the author. The only exception is brief quotations in printed reviews.

ISBN 978-1-941972-66-3

Library of Congress Control Number: 2015948146

Published by Start2Finish
Fort Worth, Texas 76244
www.start2finish.org

All Scripture quotations are from The Holy Bible, English Standard Version®, copyright © 2001 by Crossway Bibles, a publishing ministry of Good News Publishers. Used by permission. All rights reserved.

Printed in the United States of America

Cover Design: Josh Feit, Evangela.com

CONTENTS

Introduction 7

The Marks of an Effective Elder 11
   by Gregg Woodall

New Testament Pattern of Church Leadership 22
   by Jim Faughn

Qualifications for Elders 32
   by Sellers Crain

Responsibilities of Elders 44
   by Jay Lockhart

Things Elders Do That People See 53
   by Ray Bowman

Things Elders Do That People Don't See 64
   by Steve Bailey

Training Young Men to be Leaders 77
   by Howard Norton

Appointing New Elders 86
   by Jerrie Barber

The Wife of an Elder 98
   by Janace Scott

The Honor of Serving as an Elder 106
   by Ron McElyea

About the Authors 116

INTRODUCTION

Chris McCurley

On July 26, 2005, the television program *Dirty Jobs* made its debut on the Discovery Channel. The show features host Mike Rowe celebrating less-than-desirable occupations. You've heard the saying, "It's a dirty job, but someone's got to do it"? Mike Rowe's mission was to highlight the unsung heroes who did the work most people would avoid at all costs. The show appealed to a broad audience and lasted for several seasons. Viewers were both intrigued and entertained as they watched the whimsical Mike Rowe roll up his sleeves and perform the messy, the strange, and the disgusting. *Dirty Jobs* proves that, no matter how repulsive the occupation, there's always someone willing to do it.

Some would say that the role of elder in the Lord's church is a dirty job—it's a dirty job, but someone's got to do it. It is true that shepherding the flock can be messy. It can seem like a less-than-desirable position. Elders often find themselves in no-win situations. Being the spiritual leader of a flock can prove to be thankless and stress filled. Elders are appointed volunteers leading a group of volunteers. While shepherds are leaders, some members of the flock refuse to cooperate. It can be like herding butterflies. Jacob had this to say about his life as a shepherd: "By day the heat consumed me and the frost by night, and my sleep fled from my eyes" (Gen. 31:40).

Being a shepherd of the Lord's flock is not for the faint of heart. Only men of the highest moral fiber, the most distinctive character, and the utmost dedication and commitment are fit to serve in this role. This does not mean they must be perfect. If it did, no one would be qualified. However, the elder must be a man who meets the scriptural qualifications and, above all, has the heart to serve.

The biblical elder has an awesome responsibility. They have been charged with protecting the flock (Acts 20:28-31). As overseers, they are to scan the flock continuously, making sure that each and every sheep is safe. A few ways they do this is by going after sheep that have strayed, disciplining sin, and refuting false teachers. The shepherd must also feed the flock (1 Tim. 3:2). It is the duty of every elder to make certain that the members are receiving the proper nourishment. This sustenance, of course, comes from a healthy diet of God's word. The shepherd is also a steward of God's household—the local church, which means that he must lead the flock (1 Pet. 5:1-4). Shepherds do not put sheep on a leash. They do not drag the sheep. A good shepherd is one who leads by example. He has the respect of the flock. He is loving and tender, but he is also firm and direct when the occasion demands it. The godly shepherd has the trust of the flock. The sheep have confidence in his leadership because they have witnessed his submission to the Lord. The only man qualified to serve as a shepherd of the Lord's flock is the one who understands that he is not the boss. The flock does not belong to the shepherd. The flock belongs to God. Christ is the head. The shepherds are the caretakers of what has been entrusted to them; therefore, it is their duty to ensure that the flock is well taken care of.

Why would anyone want to be an elder in the Lord's church? Some assess the role and responsibility of a shepherd and are immediately turned off. While shepherding may seem like a less-than-desirable office, it is also one that affords a plethora of blessings.

INTRODUCTION

Is shepherding a dirty job? Sometimes. But it's more than a job. It's more than a duty or an obligation. Serving as an elder in the Lord's church is a privilege. It's an honor. It's the most important office a man could ever hold. It may not appeal to a wide audience, but for those who meet the qualifications and understand the responsibility, it's a task like no other.

May God bless our shepherds as they lead His sheep!

1

THE MARKS OF AN EFFECTIVE ELDER

Gregg Woodall

There have been many great books written for the business world relating to effective leadership in managing a company, but few directly relate to elders and effective shepherding of the flock. It is often said by well-meaning members that they do not want the elders to conduct the affairs of the church as if it were a commercial business enterprise. Often what drives such comments is the belief that business is cold and uncaring. However, most first-class business organizations are quite the opposite of that premise; in fact, many good business principles and practices derived their origin from the Bible.

Jesus said, "Why did you seek Me? Did you not know that I must be about My Father's business?" (Luke 2:49 NKJV). Even our Lord used the term "business" when referring to his work within the kingdom of God. While Jesus walked upon this earth, it was understood that certain business-like principles made for a good leader. Many of those privileged to serve as shepherds came from business backgrounds as leaders. I believe we would do a disservice to our congregations to abandon good leadership characteristics just because they are also found in business.

The model Jesus used to establish and build his church is one we would do well to emulate. First, he knew his mission was "to seek and to save the lost" (Luke 19:10), and that guided everything else. He then personally selected individuals to lead in this effort. He was intimately involved in their development and often sought guidance from his Father. He worked with them as a team and was their leader in accomplishing God's will. He then set in motion a plan that this was to be perpetuated until the end of time, which is where we find ourselves today.

To be an effective elder is humbling to write about. No one, myself included, has lived up to the standard of the Good Shepherd, Jesus. But I hope my thoughts on this subject will prove helpful to us as we strive to "grow in the grace and knowledge of our Lord and Savior Jesus Christ" (2 Pet. 3:18).

Stephen R. Covey's book, *The 7 Habits of Highly Effective People*, has been a top-seller for over fifteen years and has been widely used by many readers seeking to improve their effectiveness. I will not be borrowing any material from that book, except to limit my list of hallmarks to seven. Jim Collins' book, *Good to Great*, is about companies that set themselves apart by being or doing those things that make for long-lasting, well-respected businesses. One of the leading characteristics of these great companies is leaders that think and act more for the organization and its mission vs. only for themselves.

7 HALLMARKS OF AN EFFECTIVE ELDER

Self-Denial

Self-denial is easy to talk about but more difficult to practice. For a shepherd, this may mean letting others have their way over your own personal interest. Of the things we as elders make decisions about, a great many are in the realm of opinion or preference. In matters of doctrine or truth, the Lord has provided us with the answers. So it is more often than not that we may need to give preference to the wants and desires of others in matters where only personal judgment is involved. Practicing self-denial comes with the practical reward of avoiding feelings of guilt for imposing your way on others.

> And he said to all, "If anyone would come after me, let him deny himself and take up his cross daily and follow me."
> — Luke 9:23

> Let no one seek his own good, but the good of his neighbor.
> — 1 Cor. 10:24

Many times, self-denial comes in the form of inconvenience. Most of the needs and troubles needing to be dealt with don't come with a planned calendar date. More often than not, your schedule as a shepherd is subservient to the timing of others. Have you ever asked, "Why does this have to be handled right now? It is not a good time for me because I have many other matters I am struggling to complete." We need to step back and remember that, even in our own households, the needs of our families did not always come at a planned, convenient time but were usually sporadic and untimely. As an elder in the Lord's church, you must be willing to sacrifice yourself and your own interest to serve the interest of others and God. The practice of self-denial requires discipline and effort; when coupled with prayer, it can be done.

Involved in Work & Teaching

It's quite difficult to get others to follow you where you have not been or will not go. Not too long ago, my wife and I were with our church's young people on a weekend retreat that had a ropes course as part of the experience. The course was about thirty feet up in the trees and had many different challenges as you traveled from one station to the other. Sherrye and I were among the first ones to go to the stations and then assist our students as they made their way through the course. Many of the teens said that if we could do it, then they felt more comfortable to do it as well. I'll admit that we were outside of our comfort zone, but we knew we had to set the example and lead in the effort to encourage others to follow. This is true in many other aspects when it comes to encouraging others to follow your lead.

Mission efforts are another critical area where the shepherd can lead others in the work. We just returned from a mission trip on which 28 of our members went. Not only did we as the elders lead the effort, but many on the trip showed us their leadership abilities in areas where they had more skills and talents. From them, we learned to venture into areas beyond our preconceived limitations.

> And Jesus said to them, "Follow me, and I will make you become fishers of men."
> — Mark 1:17

> And what you have heard from me in the presence of many witnesses entrust to faithful men who will be able to teach others also.
> — 2 Tim. 2:2

An effective elder will do more than just make an announcement concerning a need or job to be done. He will seek out people personally and give them encouragement to participate alongside the elder in getting things done. To have followers, you must lead, which means you have to be involved in some way with every aspect of any work that is to be done. An effective elder will teach classes at all age levels within the church so as to share of himself and the Word. Among my favorite classes to teach is the high school boys and girls. Recently, all the shepherds taught a leadership class to the high school boys. We were hoping to start them thinking and planning for their future roles as leaders in the home, at work, and in the church.

Care & Timeliness

How does anyone know you care about them? One key way is to listen. Listening is not always easy. One Sunday morning, one of our young people had discussed with me at length how many cats she had around her house and how much she really cared for them. I am not a cat person, but I listened anyway—at least that morning. That Sunday night, she came to me while others around us were also talking, and I thought I heard her say something about one of her cats dying. I told her not to worry because she had plenty more at home. She looked dismayed and realized that I had not listened carefully, so she explained more emphatically that she was telling me how her grandmother had died. Boy, was I embarrassed, and needless to say, I learned to become a better listener after that!

> If a brother or sister is poorly clothed and lacking in daily food, and one of you says to them, "Go in peace, be warmed and filled," without giving them the things needed for the body, what good is that?
> — Jas. 2:15-16

> Do you not say, "There are yet four months, then comes the harvest"? Look, I tell you, lift up your eyes, and see that the fields are white for harvest.
> — John 4:35

When people are hurting or in need, it is not enough to give assurance that the issue is on the elders' agenda for the next meeting.

We need to address the matter promptly and with genuine concern. There are times when someone will be in the hospital and request that there be no visitors. However, they often do not mean for this to include the elders or ministers. In fact, most of the time, they want and expect you to be there. If you are going to make a mistake in this area, do so by showing up anyway. Frequently, visiting a member in this way creates an evangelistic opportunity to meet other family members that may not be Christians. Waiting until they are back at services is missing the mark and is too late to be effective. An effective elder will show concern and anxiousness for caring and evangelism in a way that compels others to help.

Spend Time with Members & Be Accessible

You cannot get to know members by looking at the backs of their heads in worship services. We have many fellowship meals at our congregation, and this provides an excellent opportunity to talk with and get to know folks better. But even those times are not enough. Shepherds need to host events in their homes or, if necessary, at the building to invite several folks in to form deeper relationships. How many of us would raise our children by only seeing them a few hours a week? We would consider that ridiculous. But we do this with our church family. Effective shepherds work hard to create opportunities for more intimate knowledge of their flock.

> The apostles returned to Jesus and told him all that they had done and taught.
> — Mark 6:30

> And Jesus said to him, "What do you want me to do for you?" And the blind man said to him, "Rabbi, let me recover my sight."
> — Mark 10:51

We should always be ready to listen to others and seek to understand their plight or predicament. We should be eager to be present in their time of need. Too often elders are accused of being too slow to meet a need or address a situation. As shepherds, we like to carefully and methodically deal with matters to provide for consistency and accuracy in our advice and decisions. While that sounds good and well thought out, it falls short of being there when you are needed. I am sure that you have heard it said that "Timing is everything." Well, it is not everything, but it is critical when it is you that has the need.

An effective elder does not wait to be asked for help, but makes himself available and often asks for the opportunity to help with a need. I have often referred to this as the go first anyway principle, wherein you look for those in need before they look for you. We recently had a member to lose his job and upon hearing this we went to him and offered our help should he need it. We are not going to wait for him to be in dire straits and then plead for our help. We went first anyway.

Share Life Stories

Some of the best bonding moments with members have occurred when we share our life experiences. Obviously, this requires spending time together as mentioned earlier. Once you share some of the good and bad that has happened in your life, people can better appreciate your perspective and insight about certain things. My wife and I have four wonderful married Christian children and five grandchildren. But I have experienced tragedy as well: my godly mother was killed by a drunk driver when I was just thirteen years old. My wife had breast cancer in 2007, and now we count every day as a blessing from God. Just sharing that little bit has probably given you a different perspective about whether I could be of help to you or someone you know. Sharing is important; start now.

> And he called them to him and said to them in parables, "How can Satan cast out Satan?"
> — Mark 3:23

> I am the good shepherd. I know my own and my own know me.
> — John 10:14

Jesus often used life's stories to illustrate spiritual lessons, and these were quite effective in establishing a common understanding of one another. We all have life events that have helped shape and mold us into the person we are. Sharing those with others is a very effective way to communicate a message and create a common bond. Without sharing life with each other, we are at a loss to truly know one another. An effective elder knows his members, and they know him.

Strive for Self-improvement & Growth

How often have you been impressed by something that was done well. Something as simple as eating out at a restaurant can either be a good, pleasant experience or it can leave you feeling mistreated and ignored. It is easy to see excellence, but much more effort is required to achieve it. We all work daily to improve in our business skills, improve the look of our homes and property, and even put forth an effort to look decent when we go out in public. If we can put forth the effort to grow and improve in these areas of life, why not more so in our mission as shepherds. We should also challenge our congregations to improve and grow in the grace and knowledge of our Lord Jesus Christ. If we accept mediocrity in our service to God, we will fail in being pleasing to our Father.

When people come to worship at your congregation, is it decent and in order, or is there a general state of chaos? Do those involved in publicly leading worship do so with care and concern, or do they appear to be put out with their task? Those who visit our assemblies are observing and judging our sincerity in worship, and we should strive to make a good impression. Yes, we are there to worship God, but we also are there to influence others to become faithful children of God as well. Improvement and growth require diligent planning, communicating and training for any progress to be made.

> And they were astonished beyond measure, saying, "He has done all things well. He even makes the deaf hear and the mute speak."
> — Mark 7:37

> From whom the whole body, joined and held together by every joint with which it is equipped, when each part is working properly, makes the body grow so that it builds itself up in love.
> — Eph. 4:16

Whatever we endeavor to do in life, we should do it to the best of our ability, and serving as an elder is of no less importance. Just as every member is to do their part in strengthening the body and growing, so should each elder do his part in serving within an eldership. We are not to act alone in serving as an elder, but we do have a personal obligation to carry out the mission of the Lord. We must individually and personally do our part to serve, but we must also remember that as part of the eldership (God ordained plurality), we too are subject to the eldership.

Serve

We are all familiar with the great men and women of faith

mentioned in Hebrews 11-13. Have you ever noticed that not once does it mention their faithfulness being ascribed to them for something they said or what they told to others? In every case, their faith was accounted to them for what they did. And in every case, what they did was not what they on their own decided was something they just wanted to do anyway. Do you think Noah was thrilled to spend 100 years building a boat under constant ridicule? Probably not, but he did so out of his devotion to God and willingness to obey. On and on it goes: Abraham would not have thought to sacrifice Isaac to the Lord on his own; Joshua would have rather retired than to lead a rebellious people into battle. They served God in any way he asked, and they did so willingly for the ultimate good of God's people, not for their own self-gain or interest. Being a shepherd comes with many difficulties and heartaches, but we serve because God's plan for the church includes good leaders working as His servants in the kingdom.

> The Son of Man came not to be served but to serve, and to give his life as a ransom for many.
> — Matt. 20:28

> And he sat down and called the twelve. And he said to them, "If anyone would be first, he must be last of all and servant of all."
> — Mark 9:35

Wherever there is an opportunity to serve, an effective shepherd will be the first in line to lead the way. Service requires sacrifice. An effective elder is first and foremost a servant. He is a servant of Christ, of the church, and of the eldership. We serve in the role as an elder to do just that, serve.

I have not provided these hallmarks as any indication that I have attained perfection in any of these, but if we as elders could do these things and do them well, the church would be the better for it.

Elders are charged with the ultimate responsibility of ensuring that the church of our Lord does what God has commanded it to do. An effective elder will give his greatest personal effort to make sure that this responsibility is carried out.

2

NEW TESTAMENT PATTERN OF CHURCH LEADERSHIP

Jim Faughn

On June 2, 1966, I received a high school diploma from the now non-existent Metropolis Community High School in Metropolis, Illinois. My goal at that time was to become a lawyer. However, while pursuing an undergraduate degree, I decided that even more schooling beyond that was not for me—at least not at that time. I changed my mind (but not my major) and took courses necessary to be certified to teach in Illinois.

When the academic year began at my old high school in 1970, I was there in an entirely new role. I was no longer a member of the student body; I was on the faculty. It was a little strange to sit in the teachers' lounge and attend meetings with some who had been my teachers but were now my colleagues. It was also strange (and somewhat disconcerting) to learn of "educational politics." It did not take long to realize that such a thing existed. Some of it was not pretty.

During my eight year tenure as a high school teacher, I was baptized into Christ. When I did that, I left the religious denomination in which I was reared, one that had a "pastor system." While I did not understand all that was involved in that, I knew my father was a deacon in that church and that the deacons did the "hiring and firing" of preachers. What seemed odd to me was that once the preacher (pastor) was hired, he became in effect the CEO of the local church. To be sure, an individual congregation answered to a local, state, and national group, but the preacher was expected to run the local "day-to-day operations."

As a part of my conversion to Christ and becoming a member of his church, I learned that the "system" I had been accustomed to all of my life did not follow the pattern of the New Testament. One example of that is that I do not remember ever hearing about elders in the denomination I left. The term "pastor" was always used in reference to the preacher. As a part of the teaching that led to my conversion to Christ, I learned that, according to the New Testament, there are several pastors in a local congregation. There is no justification for referring to only one man as the pastor (cf. Acts 20:17ff; Phil. 1:1). I also learned that these men could also be referred to as bishops, elders, and presbyters. There are a number of passages that demonstrate this truth, but I will refer to only one here.

In Acts 20, Paul met at Miletus with the elders of the church at Ephesus (v. 17). In v. 28, he charged them to "feed" or "care for" the church. The word translated "feed" or "care for" is the verb form of the word from which we get our word "pastor." In that same verse, Paul reminded these men that they were "overseers" of the church at Ephesus. The Greek word translated "overseers" can also be rendered as "bishops." Since these same men may be properly referred to in these different ways, these terms may be used interchangeably during the remainder of this chapter.

The following was not the case in the denomination which I left, but it is definitely the case in many others. Many religious group refer to only one man in a specific congregation as the bishop or refer to one man who is "over" several congregations in that manner. There is no biblical justification for such a practice.

As I continued to study, I learned that the New Testament gave specific qualifications for those men who wanted to serve the Lord and the local congregation in this way. As I studied those qualifications given by the Holy Spirit and recorded by Paul in 1 Tim. 3 and Tit. 1, I learned that the "system" I left had many more flaws than just the one-man pastor system. One of those flaws has to do with what might be called the "family qualifications" which must be met by each man who serves as an elder/bishop/pastor. The Holy Spirit's instructions are that these men are to be "the husband of one wife, and his children are believers" (Tit. 1:6). In the denomination I left, it is possible for a single man with no children to serve as a "pastor." It is also possible for a married man with no children to do the same.

In those days when I was studying my way out of denominationalism and into the Lord's church, I was curious. I wanted to learn all I could about the scriptural ways of doing things. Because of my background, you might say I refused to accept things merely because somebody (even an elder, a preacher, or a family member) said it. Again, allow me to stress that a part of my devotion to the Lord, even now, is an attempt to follow the New Testament. It is my prayer that I am following in the footsteps of those wonderful Bereans who "received the word with all eagerness, examining the Scriptures daily to see if these things were so" (Acts 17:11).

For that reason, the remainder of this chapter may not be quite what some might expect to read in a discussion about the New Testament pattern for church leadership. It is not my intention at all to upset the applecart; I am not trying to be confrontational or controversial in any way. Those who know me well would testify to the fact that this really is not a part of my nature.

I am also not suggesting that I have some "new insight" that has been hidden from others for centuries. What I hope to do is present something that is much closer to the New Testament pattern than the denomination I left. It is also my observation that it could be beneficial to many congregations of the Lord's church. Many of us may have borrowed more concepts from the world than we might realize.

NEW TESTAMENT PATTERN OF CHURCH LEADERSHIP   25

Each of us must examine what happens in our local congregations and compare it with what we find in the New Testament.

As we begin, I would like to once again refer to my former occupation. I would also like to examine whether any comparisons can be made with that "system" and what may be true among us. In most school systems, the local community elects a school board. The role of that board is to determine such things as budgets, policies, etc. The school board will also hire a superintendent, one or more principals, and other staff. The role of these individuals is to carry out the desires of the community as represented by the school board. If and when the community and/or the school board becomes dissatisfied with how things are going, one or more member(s) of the administration and staff become(s) expendable or may be reassigned to another role. If the dissatisfaction becomes extremely great, there may be a complete overhaul of the school board itself.

Honestly, is this not a parallel to how some people view church leadership? Does our thinking not bear some similarity to the educational model, or maybe even the corporate model with a board, a CEO, an organizational chart, etc.? Is it not true that, in at least some congregations, there is some sort of process for the selection of elders by the members of the congregation? As one listens to many of the prayers in our assemblies, is it not also true that many of those prayers are for the elders as "they make decisions"? Isn't it also true that one of the most important decisions the elders are expected to make is the selection of those who will serve in various capacities in the local congregation? This seems to be especially true with regard to whomever they choose to occupy the pulpit. It also seems to be true that this person is to do much more than occupy the pulpit on Sunday; he is expected, along with other "paid staff" and volunteers, to keep things running smoothly throughout the week. When dissatisfaction grows, one or more things will likely happen. It may be that the solution is to send the preacher packing. It may be that there will be a call for a change in the eldership. It may be that people will leave in order to find a congregation more to their liking. Any number of things can happen. Any number of things has happened in far too many congregations.

For that reason, I would like to make some suggestions for your consideration. Again, these suggestions may not be what one might expect to read in a chapter like this. However, they are both scriptural and practical.

First, "church leadership" is not limited to a group of men who wear specific titles. Let me be clear; when a congregation is scripturally organized, there will be both bishops/elders/pastors and deacons in that congregation (cf. Phil. 1:1). Further, while every Christian is a minister, there are those who, like Timothy, may wear the designation of "minister" (cf. 1 Thess. 3:2; 1 Tim. 4:6). I do not mean to imply that there is no need for men to serve in these capacities, or that the biblical designations are outdated.

At the same time, I believe "church leadership" is not limited to these men. A person can lead a Bible class without being an elder, deacon, or preacher. In fact, one of the best Bible teachers we have where I preach and serve as an elder is not, has never been, and will never be an elder or deacon. Since he and his wife have never had children and are beyond the age of ever having children, he does not meet the biblical requirements for either position. But anyone who sits in a class he leads is blessed. It is also the case that he and his wife involve themselves in service to other (primarily younger) couples in an effort to lead them to a better understanding of God's will. Almost always this is done without "fanfare" and with a humble attempt to help lead people to heaven.

Both the list of leaders in a local congregation and the ways in which they lead is almost inexhaustible. Parents are to lead children. Older women are to lead younger women. Older couples can lead younger couples. Teens can lead pre-teens. The list of "leaders" can go on and on. There are also any number of ways by which leadership is done. Leading can be done by formal instruction, informal instruction, example, and in a host of other ways.

Second, the fact that elders are expected to be "overseers" is both biblical and weighty. "Remember your leaders, those who spoke to you the word of God. Consider the outcome of their way of life, and imitate their faith" (Heb. 13:7). As I consider daily my responsibilities as an elder, I turn often to 1 Tim. 3 and Tit. 1, and I try to evaluate myself in terms of what I read there about the qualifications for this work.

What you are about to read is, in no way, a criticism of anybody else. It is not meant to introduce "some new thing" into the discussion of church leadership. Rather, the following are the thoughts of a very imperfect man who struggles everyday to follow the perfect example and who asks for your prayers as he does so. When I think of the New Testament pattern for church leadership, I remember that the New Testament was written centuries before the "corporate model" became the norm. Our Lord and the apostles did not live during a time when boards (corporate, educational, or otherwise) were common. To be sure, both the Roman government and the Jewish religious system had firmly entrenched and highly organized systems. But as I read the New Testament, I find little evidence that our Lord's "model" for church leadership followed such systems. As I consider my role as an elder, and as I think about biblical leadership on any level, my mind focuses on the One who said, "I am the good shepherd" (John 10:11). Accordingly, I humbly submit for your consideration my take on the New Testament pattern for church leadership. It seems to me that, if I am to use the Lord's model as my "pattern" for leadership, the following concepts (all taken from John 10) will be very apparent:

Communication

Those I am trying to lead will hear my voice (v. 3). It is my firm conviction that this is best done in informal, maybe even personal, settings. The communication suggested here does not sound to me at all like a "pronouncement from on high," but the voice of a friend.

Leadership

A leader leads (vv. 3-4). I know that sounds redundant, but is it? Aren't leaders often perceived as giving orders and sending others into the fray instead of "leading the charge" themselves? Whatever I desire to see in others needs to also be a part of my life. If I want the congregation where I serve to be more evangelistic, my brethren must also see me as evangelistic. If I want the congregation to be more loving, I must be more loving. The list can go on and on, but you get the idea. The old idea of "Do as I say, not as I do" won't work. The Chief Shepherd left us His example, and elders must in turn be "examples to the flock" (1 Pet. 5:3).

Commitment

Those who follow the Lord's pattern for leadership are not in it for the money (cf. John 10:12), for prestige, or for any other similar reason. Such a man is to be committed to the Lord, to his task of shepherding God's flock (1 Peter 5:2). God's people need leaders upon whom they can depend through thick and thin.

Sacrifice

The time may not come when a leader is called upon to lay "down his life for the sheep" (John 10:11), but a leader will sacrifice resources, time, energy, sleep, and a host of other things because of his concern for, and love of, the people under his oversight. Real concern for the welfare of others—the Chief Shepherd said, "I came that they may have life and have it abundantly" (John 10:10). Those who wish to follow Jesus' example will be concerned with upholding the truth of God's Word. Elders have absolutely no authority to change God's plan of salvation, how to worship properly, the way in which his people are to be organized, the mission of the church, or any of a number of other things.

At the same time, a shepherd will remember that "godliness is of value in every way, as it holds promise for the present life and also for the life to come" (1 Tim. 4:8). It needs to be remembered that one of the wonderful things mentioned in Psa. 23 about the Lord and his role as David's Shepherd is, "He leads me in paths of righteousness for his name's sake" (v. 3).

A real concern for the welfare of others will involve encouraging people when they are headed in the right direction, while discouraging them when their behavior, beliefs, and/or lifestyles have the real potential to be detrimental to them in this life, as well as in the one to come.

Relationship

This is the glue that holds everything together. The leader will not only know the followers "as a group"—he will also be able to call "his own sheep *by name*" (John 10:3, emphasis added). This can also be said about those who are following this pattern: "I know my own and my own know me" (v. 14). Later, Jesus said, "My sheep hear my voice, and I know them, and they follow me" (v. 27).

One of the saddest statements I have ever heard about an eldership involved this point. A preacher I know was talking to a young lady about something that was troubling her. When he suggested she talk to their shepherds about this, her comment was: "I am not walking into a room full of strangers to talk about this."

There's something wrong with that picture. The fault may have been hers. She may not have wanted to develop a relationship with the elders. The fault may have been theirs. They may have operated out of a "board of director" mindset. I am not a member of that congregation, so I have no way of knowing where the fault lies. I am confident, though, that this situation could be a lot better than it seems to be. Neither an elder nor a member of a congregation needs to be viewed as a stranger!

At this point, we will leave our discussion of John and turn to one other passage for the remaining points I would like to make. Both of them are found in 1 Pet. 5:4.

Accountability

It must never be forgotten that there is One who is the Chief Shepherd (1 Pet. 5:4). The congregation in which I am a member does not belong to me. Directions are not to be determined by a popular vote. "The way we've always done things" is not the yardstick. Each of us, including leaders, "must all appear before the judgment seat of Christ, so that each one may receive what is due for what he has done in the body, whether good or evil" (2 Cor. 5:10).

Reward

The same verse that mentions the Chief Shepherd also mentions "the unfading crown of glory." The church secretary where I once preached made something for me to put in my office. The message was: "Working for the Lord doesn't pay much, but the retirement plan is out of this world." I think that pretty well sums it up.

I will close this discussion by asking you to do two things that, to me, are very important. First, I ask that you consider carefully what I have written here. The words that you have read are not intended to point a finger, be critical, remake the brotherhood, or have any negative effect on the greatest cause the world has ever known. They have been an attempt to help all of us glorify God.

Secondly, I would ask you to pray for me as I try to fulfill my God-given responsibility and privilege as one of many leaders of his people.

3

QUALIFICATIONS FOR ELDERS

Sellers Crain

One of the most critical problems we face in the church today is a shortage of men who are qualified and willing to serve as elders. We need Christian men who are willing to prepare themselves to be elders, and we need congregations to encourage that preparation and provide some kind of training for such a work. To help with this training, congregations could provide the chance for these men to prove themselves, possibly by serving as deacons first and giving them a variety of assignments in every aspect of the church's work. How helpful it would be to a congregation to have men willing and ready to serve when the opportunity presents itself!

Why do we need elders anyway? The answer to that question is found in the Bible where we can find that the organization of the church is God's plan, and it cannot be improved upon (Acts 20:28; Phil. 1:1; 1 Tim. 3:1-7; Tit. 1:5-9; 1 Pet. 5:1-4). Furthermore, the qualifications for men to serve as elders are not incidental; they are absolute and inspired of God (2 Tim. 3:16-17). We can also read of the example of Paul as he appointed elders in every church he established and commanded Titus to "appoint elders in every city" (Tit. 1:5; Acts 14:23).

In over 50 years in ministry, I can't recall a time that I did not have respect for my elders, and I was humbled when my elders where I preached for 24 years asked me to serve with them. I preached for over 45 years before being appointed as an elder. That experience provided me with the sense of the burden of responsibility that accompanies the position of an elder. When my name was put forward, the only objection raised was that, since I was the preacher, I would have too much power. When my elders revealed that to me (without giving me the name of the objector), my answer to them was, "That says more about him than it does about me because I do not see the eldership as a power position. It is a position of service." Carl Spain wrote that it is an "office of service."[1] Burton Coffman also expresses that idea by writing, "Paul calls the office a good work, which shows that an elder has something on his shoulders besides holding an office."[2]

How often have you heard this prayer, "Lord, help our elders in making decisions"? Certainly that is one of the many responsibilities elders have. The words *elder* and *presbyter* refer to that decision-making responsibility. I have not always agreed with the elders I have served with, but I have never disagreed with their scriptural right to make decisions. I consider it my obligation to support their decisions as long as they do not in any way violate God's Word. Elders are not lawmakers. "There is only one lawgiver and judge, he who is able to save and to destroy," and that is Jesus Christ (Jas. 4:12). In matters of faith, elders must make their decisions based on "thus saith the Lord." Even in matters of "opinion" or "expediency," they have the responsibility to make decisions. Such decisions should always be made in keeping with scriptural principles and with the welfare of the congregation they serve in mind. Elders will make mistakes; when they do, they should be accepted as human errors.

Members should submit to the oversight of their elders (Heb. 13:7, 17). When we have men of faith, vision, and a love for God, for their sheep, and for the lost, we should willingly and eagerly follow their leadership. Good leadership demands good "followership." Burton Coffman wrote an article entitled "An Elder is a Man." In this article, he acknowledged there are times when elders must show special courage in their leadership; his main points were:

- An elder is a man, subject to errors of judgment. Yet, he must go ahead with courage to make decisions, knowing he could be wrong. It is not possible to know 100% of all things before a decision is made.

- An elder is a man, enjoying the approval of those he leads. Yet, he must have the courage to make decisions based upon his spiritual and intellectual judgment, knowing it may cost him the favor of the church.

- An elder is a husband, aware of the frailty of the human family. Yet, he must proceed with courage in leadership, knowing his family will, by association, fall heir to some criticism directed at him.

- An elder is a man, a student of mankind and time. Yet, he cannot remain simply a student; he must be a teacher, knowing the ultimate direction of the church and its growth in the future depends upon his reactions today.

- An elder is a man, conscious of his responsibility. Yet, he must have the courage to trust others with responsibility... knowing that they may fumble, they may quit, or they may ignore the assignment.

- An elder is a man, awed by the power of God. Yet, his love for the souls of men causes him to accept the office of a bishop, knowing that someday he will stand in God's presence and give account of his own dealings with those he was to lead.

Coffman closes by saying, "It is likely that no man on earth would accept the challenge of leading as an elder, if God had not promised wisdom from above and inner strength of character that comes from His eternal presence."

A critical period in the life of any church is when elders are being selected. My experience has taught me that this is true regardless of whether it is choosing elders for the first time or choosing men to serve with the current eldership. Three mistakes should be avoided when choosing men to serve as elders. The first mistake to avoid is selecting men just so you can have elders. Having no elders is preferable to having the wrong kind (unqualified and nonspiritual men).

The second mistake to avoid is making the qualifications so difficult that no one could measure up to them. Elders are not perfect men; they are not superhuman; they are not divine; they are just human. The qualifications laid out in Scripture do not call for perfection, but they do call for men who have prepared themselves and who are spiritually qualified. Sometimes I fear when we are selecting elders, we grab for our calendars (how old is he), and our calculators (how many children does he have), and the scriptural and spiritual qualifications are forgotten. Aren't a man's spiritual qualifications more important than his chronological age? Isn't the kind of father he is more important than how many children he has? I am not saying these things should not be considered, but we must not make them more important than the spiritual qualifications. A failure to follow the Bible's instructions about the need for qualified men to serve the church as elders has been one source of heartache and division within the body of Christ.

The third mistake to avoid is appointing men to do the work of elders (committees, men's business meetings, etc.) instead of appointing qualified men as elders. This approach is an attempt to circumvent God's teaching on elders. Franklin Camp wrote, "Selecting elders is in some ways like a marriage. It is either done right or the consequences may last a lifetime. The direction of the congregation will be determined by the kind of men who are selected as elders. The selection of the right kind of men can start a congregation on a course of spiritual growth and development that will mean the salvation of many souls and bring glory to God. The selection of the wrong kind of men can stifle the growth of the church, and it will be a constant source of strife and friction.[3]

No congregation will ever rise above its leaders. Flavil Yeakley wrote that, "Every bottleneck that I have ever seen was at the top of the bottle."[4]

WHAT ARE AN ELDER'S QUALIFICATIONS?

In his instructions to Timothy, Paul begins by saying if a man "aspires to the office of overseer, he desires a noble task" (1 Tim. 3:1). It is debated about whether or not this is a qualification. It is clear that if a man does not desire the work, he should not be appointed. Desire speaks of motivation, and Peter said he must be willing to serve, "not under compulsion, but willingly" (1 Pet. 5:2). A willingness to serve should be the main desire of one seeking the position of an elder. Flavil Yeakley pointed out that there are two different Greek words translated "'desire' (epithumeo; orego), and they are both used in this text."[5] The first of these words means to "earnestly and eagerly desire" something. The second word means "to stretch forward, long for or seek." Yeakley added that "the office should seek the man and not the man seeking the office." A man should express a desire to serve as an elder, but he should not campaign for the office.

Burton Coffman wrote that the "requirement of having to first be proved (or tested), which is given for those being considered as deacons, was also mandatory in the case of the elders."[6] In quoting from Lenski, who was in agreement with his statement, Coffman wrote, "The fact that such a testing was to be applied to overseers is so self-evident from the conditions laid down in 1 Tim. 3:2-8, that 'also' now refers to it."[7] The eldership is not a training or testing program. The men who are selected should be those who have previously proven themselves to be men of spiritual character and discipline and who are willing to serve.

Instead of examining the qualifications individually as is usually done, for the purposes of this study, we will examine them in groups.

Temperament

Men who are selected to serve as elders should be those of the right disposition (1 Tim. 3:2-3). They should be men who are self-controlled in all areas of life. This nature is further expressed in being of good behavior, gentle, not quarrelsome, hot tempered, or one easily angered (Tit. 1:7).

A Family Man

A man selected to be an elder should be a family man. One who is the "husband of one wife," meaning having only one living wife. If he has previously had a wife who is deceased, and he has scripturally remarried (Matt. 19:9), he can serve as an elder. This qualification rules out a homosexual from serving, although he may be a Christian if he is not practicing that lifestyle (1 Cor. 6:9-11). The requirement of an elder to be the "husband of one wife" also eliminates women from being elders, but they can and do serve in many other ways. This man should also be one who guides his household well. His children must believe, be in submission to him, and not be insubordinate (1 Tim. 3:4-5; Tit. 1:6). They must not be those who are accused of "riotous or unruly" conduct or dispositions. Yeakley wrote, "What is required is that the young children be in subjection and that those who are old enough to be Christians actually are faithful Christians-preferably throughout their lives, but at least for so long a time as they are part of that man's household. The key here is parental control and responsibility, not place of residence."[8]

An elder should be a spiritually mature man and "not a novice." While this phrase can mean one who is not a new convert, it can also apply to one who has not matured in the faith (1 Tim. 3:6; cf. 1 Pet. 2:2; Heb. 5:12-14). A spiritually mature man is less likely to let his appointment to the eldership go to his head. In relationship to this point, he must not be "self-willed" (Tit. 1:7) If a man of this disposition is appointed, in most cases it will be affected by his own prejudices, opinions, and judgments. This can also affect his vision which could become the automatic boundaries for the church's progress. An elder should have very strong convictions, but he should also be able to see the different points of view discussed by the other elders. One man cannot rule the roost. There is only one man who is the ruler in the truest sense of the word, and that is Jesus Christ. No other man qualifies for that position. When elders are said to rule, it refers to leading and guiding (Heb. 13:7, 17).

I once worked with a congregation whose elders told me they did not agree on anything unless all of them agreed. When told that I responded by saying, "One monkey does not stop the show," and added, "If that is the way you make decisions, then one man can rule the roost." God's Word calls for a plurality of elders and not a one man show. Ira North mentioned in his book *Balance* that when he worked with the Madison Church of Christ in Madison, TN, the preachers and the elders had an understanding: "Everybody had his say, but nobody had his way."

Having a Good Name

When a man is being considered for the eldership, he should be one having a good reputation. The word "blameless" is used in this regard (1 Tim. 3:2; Tit. 1:6-7). No person can be completely without fault in every conceivable way. It has been suggested that this refers to being blameless in the things that were previously mentioned. In his letter to Titus, Paul adds the thought of being irreproachable, meaning that if a charge is brought against this man, it is one that cannot be substantiated (1:6-7). In this same connection, this man is to "be well thought of by outsiders" (1 Tim. 3:7). However, this must not be understood as allowing people outside the church to judge those within the church (1 Cor. 5:12-13). Someone who is being considered as an elder should be known in his community as a man of good moral character, of love, kindness, generosity, and goodness. If he does not have the respect from the people among whom he lives, to appoint him to the eldership would lead to reproach on Christ and his body, the church.

Not a Drunkard

An elder should not be a drinker of alcohol (1 Tim. 3:3; Tit. 1:7). Drunkenness was just as much a real problem in that age as it is now. The drinking of alcoholic beverages has been a matter of disagreement and debate throughout the history of the church. One thing that is not debated is that drunkards, along with other sinners, "will not inherit the kingdom of God" (1 Cor. 6:9; cf. Gal. 5:21). Paul wrote to the Ephesians, "Do not get drunk with wine, for that is debauchery, but be filled with the Spirit," (5:18). While this passage refers to Christians in general, elders must remain apart from any evil influences and set an example of sobriety for others to follow. The Old Testament condemns drunkenness (Prov. 20:1; 23:29-35), and spiritual leaders were to abstain from wine because of their position, example, and influence. Priests could not enter the house of God while under the influence of alcohol (Lev. 10:9). Kings were advised not to consume wine because it could hamper their judgment (Prov. 31:4-5). Nazarites, those who had taken the highest spiritual vow in that day and time, were forbidden to drink wine (Num. 6:3; cf. Judg. 13:4-5; 1 Sam. 1:11). Does it not seem reasonable that spiritual leaders today should exercise the same discipline so they can be responsible in their judgment and set the example of being a Spirit-controlled person?

A Student of God's Word

Any man who is asked to serve as an elder should be a man of the book and a student of God's Word. Paul said that he must be "able to teach" (1 Tim. 3:2). This means that he is one who is "fitted, suitable, and ready" to teach. This does not imply that he must be teaching all of the time, but that he is capable of teaching if he is called upon. Some scholars understand Paul's words in the Ephesian letter, that God gave some to be "pastors and teachers" to be one function vs. two different ones. They consider this passage to speak of pastors (elders) who are teachers (Eph. 4:11). David Lipscomb and J. W. Shepherd commented on this text, "Those endowed to feed and teach those already Christians the duties and obligations resting on them as children of God."[9] John MacArthur explains how these functions work together when he writes:

> Teachers has to do with the primary function of pastors... Though teaching can be identified as a ministry on its own (1 Cor. 12:28), pastors and teachers are best understood as one office of leadership in the church... the text of 1 Timothy 5:17 clearly puts the two functions together when it says, "Let the elders who rule well be considered worthy of double honor, especially those who work hard at preaching and teaching"... Those two functions define the teaching shepherd.[10]

While public or private teaching is not specified, this man should be able to "feed the flock" (Acts 20:20; 1 Pet. 5:2). He should know the Bible well enough that he can "exhort and convince the gainsayers" (Tit. 1:9-11).

Neal Pollard wrote an article entitled "The Kind of Elders I Want to Follow." He said that man was one who is:

1. A spiritual man, whose heart, concern, and life centers around the cross.

2. A genuine man, lacking pretentiousness and political savvy, who loves people.

3. A compassionate man, not unable to shed tears and show emotion over important things (souls, not sports; praise, not politics; members, not movies or money, etc).

4. An imperfect man, who though spiritually mature, understands I am weak and human, and who is himself human.

5. An approachable man, who garners respect—not through gruffness and intimidation, and who at the same time is warm and welcoming.

6. A sound man, who demonstrates the ability to discern between truth and error and whose love for God will cause him to defend vigorously His church and doctrine without partiality.

7. A loving man, who demonstrates this at every level—spousal, family, community, church, and God.

8. An active man, who does not participate aloofly in the work of the church, but whose sleeves are rolled up and whose efforts help make the church great.

9. A sensitive man, not prone to be overly hasty or habitually lethargic, who deliberates, weighs, considers, and decides upon matters with wisdom and maturity.

10. A qualified man, not by my heightened or hypercritical standards, who meets—though none ever will to perfection—those stated qualifications in Timothy and Titus.

Conclusion

Elders "watch over your souls" (Heb. 13:17). As discussed earlier, they do have a decision-making responsibility as well as an administrative responsibility. The terms bishop and overseer mean that one of their responsibilities is to administrate the aspects of the church's business. Unfortunately, sometimes this aspect dominates elderships, and the shepherding goes undone. While I do believe elders have the responsibility to be good stewards of God's money, they are never told to watch for money, but they are told to watch for souls. Jesus is the Good Shepherd (John 10:11). In his discussion of that role, he said,

> But he who enters by the door is the shepherd of the sheep. To him the gatekeeper opens. The sheep hear his voice, and he calls his own sheep by name and leads them out. When he has brought out all his own, he goes before them, and the sheep follow him, for they know his voice. A stranger they will not follow, but they will flee from him, for they do not know the voice of strangers. The thief comes only to steal and kill and destroy. I came that they may have life and have it abundantly.
> — John 10:2-5, 10

Those now serving as elders, and those who desire to be elders, need to learn from Him and follow His example.

Notes

1. Carl Spain, *Commentary on 1 and 2 Timothy and Titus* (Austin: Sweet), 53.
2. James Burton Coffman, *Commentary on 1 & 2 Thessalonians, 1& 2 Timothy, Titus & Philemon* (Austin, TX: Firm Foundation, 1978), 174.
3. Franklin Camp, *Leadership Principles, Personalities and Practice*, 15.
4. Flavil Yeakley, *Church Leadership and Organization* (Nashville: Christian Communications, 1980), 17.
5. Ibid., 116.
6. Coffman, *Commentary*, 152.
7. Ibid., 153.
8. Yeakley, *Church Leadership*, 119.
9. David Lipscomb and J. W. Shepherd, *A Commentary on the New Testament Epistles: Ephesians, Philippians, and Colossians* (Nashville: Gospel Advocate, 1976), 78.
10. John MacArthur, *Ephesians* (Chicago: Moody, 1986), 143.

4

RESPONSIBILITIES OF ELDERS

Jay Lockhart

When Jesus promised to build His church (Matt. 16:18), Matthew used a Greek word, *ekklēsia*, which is translated "church." It is a compound word meaning "out of" (*ek*) and "to call" (*kaleō*). In the word itself, we are not told who is called out, how they are called out, or why they are called out. In the New Testament, the word always refers to people. While it is used to describe Israel being called out of Egypt (Acts 7:38) and certain people being called out to defend the goddess Diana (Artemis) (Acts 19:32), the word most commonly refers to the people of God who have been called out of the world by the gospel (2 Thess. 2:14). They are people who, in obedience to the gospel, have been added to the body of Christ (Acts 2:47; Eph. 1:22-23), who honor the authority of Christ as the one head of the body (Col. 1:18), who are reconciled to God (Eph. 2:16), and who are saved by Christ (Eph. 5:23). These called out people are the universal church which belongs to Christ.

We learn from the teaching of Scripture that the church was planted throughout the Roman world in local congregations to worship and serve Christ. The organization of the church is summarized in Phil. 1:1 when Paul addressed his letter "To all the saints in Christ Jesus who are at Philippi, with the overseers and deacons." In fully developed congregations, there were a plurality of bishops (also called elders or shepherds) who met specific qualifications set forth in 1 Tim. 3:1-7, and Tit. 1:5-9; there were special deacons (servants) who met the qualifications of 1 Tim. 3:8-10, 12-13; and there were the saints (the other members of the congregation, including the evangelists). The church was organized so that each congregation was autonomous in its subjection to the authority of Christ. There was no state, national, or international organization in the New Testament church. This lesson will emphasize the work of elders in the local church.

1. The work of elders as seen in the terms used.

There are several different terms used in Scripture that refer to the office we most commonly call elder. While each term refers to the same position, we can see different responsibilities of this office highlighted when we examine the meanings of each word. The term elder (*presbuteros*) refers to one older and mature in the Christian faith (Acts 14:23; Tit. 1:5; Acts 20:17). Elders in the church should develop two things which can come only with age: experience and wisdom. Age does bring experience, and although it is not a guarantee, age should also bring wisdom. While youth has many things going for it (vigor, vitality, excitement), experience and wisdom come only with age. As men of experience and wisdom, elders are equipped to counsel members of the local church in countless areas of their lives such as: how to be good husbands/fathers and wives/mothers, how to be faithful in the service of Christ, how to choose vocations, the proper use of finances, where to attend college, how to grow old gracefully, how to handle disappointments, and many others.

The term bishop or overseer (*episkopos*) means "to watch over, to be near, to care for" (Acts 20:28). Elders can be mentors to people in the congregation. They can help those members grow spiritually towards the goal of developing into the image of Christ.

The term shepherd (*poimēn*) means pastor or shepherd (Acts 20:28). As shepherds, these men are to lead the church by providing the vision for the church to accomplish its God-given mission. They are also to feed the church through teaching. While the elders are not required to do all of the teaching, they are responsible for all that is taught in the congregation. Therefore, they should know what is being taught in Bible classes and monitor what is taught from the pulpit, insisting that teachers and preachers teach only the truth and "the whole counsel of God" (Acts 20:27).

In the course of time, teaching should include how to be saved, the nature of the New Testament church, how the church is to worship, the roles of men and women in the church, and what is to be included and excluded in living a faithful Christian life. Many problems in the local church can be avoided if elders will expect more of themselves and of the teachers and preachers. As shepherds, these men are also to protect the church from all harmful threats to the sheep from within and without. To do this, they must be able to distinguish between truth and error (Tit. 1:9). Elders must take seriously their work as shepherds, knowing that they "must give account" (Heb. 13:17) for the way they perform their work.

The term ruler (*proistēmi*) means "to stand before, to be over, to take the lead" (1 Thess. 5:12). Elders are to model the Christian life in every respect. Peter said that elders are to "be examples to the flock" (1 Pet. 5:3).

The term leader (*hēgeomai*) means "to lead, guide, govern" (Heb. 13:7, 17). Elders should remember that they lead by consent, and therefore, they are not "lords over" the flock (1 Pet. 5:3). People choose the congregation in which they will worship and serve, and elders cannot force people to do their will. As leaders, elders must seek the will of Christ in all matters of faith (1 Pet. 4:11), and they would be wise to seek the will of the people in matters of opinion.

Loving persuasion is a great quality for an elder to possess.

To summarize the work of elders by the terms used in the New Testament, we would say that elders are to be mentors, counselors, shepherds (who lead, feed, and protect), models, and leaders. Let elders be examples who inspire, shields who protect, and guides who lead the flock to greater faithfulness and growth.

2. The work of elders as seen in the qualifications given.

The qualifications for elders which are set forth in 1 Timothy 3 and Titus 1 are not merely suggestions as to the type man who should serve. It is essential for every man who serves as an elder to have some sign of all the qualifications given in Scriptures. He will be stronger in some areas than in others, but if he has some sign of every qualification he can grow in the areas where he needs to improve. Congregations should never possess an attitude of settling for finding the best men available without considering the scriptural qualifications.

The qualifications for elders suggest certain areas of his work. First, an elder's work begins with himself. To the elders of the church in Ephesus Paul said, "Take heed to yourselves" (Acts 20:28). If a man "desires the position" of an elder (1 Tim. 3:1), let him work hard to meet the qualifications. In looking to himself, an elder has domestic responsibilities: he is to be a faithful husband and a respected father "who rules his own house well, having his children in submission with all reverence" (1 Tim. 3:4). An elder has social responsibilities: he is to be a good and gentle man, self-controlled, hospitable, easy to be entreated, just, and a man who has a good reputation in his community. An elder has spiritual responsibilities: he is to avoid covetousness, be sober-minded, be holy, love what is good, and hold to sound doctrine. He is to be a man of God. Secondly, the elder is to look to his congregation. An elder with these qualifications is well equipped to do the work assigned by God as an elder, an overseer, and a shepherd. Let elders communicate well with the church, and the church will follow men with these qualifications.

3. The work of elders as seen in their responsibilities.

Elders are to "take heed to all the flock" as they serve as "overseers" (Acts 20:28; 1 Pet. 5:2). Some people question whether elders have authority. Let it be remembered that every command of God carries the authority to do whatever is necessary to obey that command. God commands elders to take the oversight. Therefore, they have the authority to do what is necessary to be overseers. They have authority over all the work of the church. What the local church does and what it becomes is the responsibility of the elders.

4. The work of the elders as seen in their leading by consent.

The church is not a corporation with a CEO who "calls the shots" and controls employees by job security and a pay check. Members of the church belong to a local congregation by free choice. No Christian should consider himself to be "a member at large," but in keeping with the Lord's will, he should work in a local congregation under the oversight of the elders of that church if it is fully organized. In leading by consent, elders understand that they are not to be lords over the church (1 Pet. 5:3), but are to provide leadership by persuasion. In matters of faith, elders must prayerfully seek direction from Scripture and present a united front to the congregation. In matters of opinion, wise elders will seek the will of the people and work very hard to "maintain the unity of the Spirit in the bond of peace" (Eph. 4:3). The congregation should accept a consensus of the leadership without being contentious (Tit. 3:10). Both leaders and members should remember in all matters that God's goal for each of us is to develop into the image of Christ (Rom. 8:29).

5. The work of elders as seen in their vision and faith.

The vision of the local church will never rise above the vision of its leaders. Elders should formulate a "vision statement" for the church that should contain the goal of Christ for the church and the world (Matt. 28:18-20). Additionally, leaders should have a written and well-known "mission statement" that states how the local church plans to fulfill the vision of Christ for the world. Finally, the church should have a "theme statement" each year that spells out specifically how the congregation plans to fulfill its vision and mission in the next twelve months. As elders lead in capturing a vision for the church, they should have faith enough to make plans that are beyond the known ability of the congregation to fulfill on its own. It is a lack of faith to plan only as far as we can see. We need to leave room for God "to do far more abundantly than all that we ask or think, according to the power at work within us" (Eph. 3:20). Let us make big plans for God's work.

6. The work of elders as seen in their setting the right kind of example.

Peter said elders are to be "examples to the flock" (1 Pet. 5:3). Successful leaders will live in such a way that they may say by their actions, "Be imitators of me, as I am of Christ" (1 Cor. 11:1). Here are some areas in which elders should be great examples: respect for the authority of Scripture, helping the church to depend upon prayer, promoting the spirit of love and unity in the congregation, involvement in and active support for the work programs of the church, evangelism and edification, and ministering to the sheep of their flock.

7. The work of the elders as seen in their decision making.

Elders are more than decision makers, but they must make many decisions. How do they make good decisions? First, they should consult the Scriptures to find any teaching which relates to the decision either by direct statements or by principles. Obviously, the Bible will not specifically address every decision that must be made. Second, let elders pray for wisdom (Jas. 1:5) that they may make good decisions. Third, let elders seek the advice of spiritually strong individuals within the congregation and a consensus from the congregation itself. Fourth, they should take as much time as is reasonable in making decisions, especially major ones. Fifth, they should weigh all of the alternatives and the consequences of each one. Sixth, after moving through the first five steps, they are ready to make the decision and trust God for the outcome.

8. The work of the elders as seen in equipping the saints.

Paul stated that the work of church leadership was "to equip the saints for the work of ministry, for building up the body of Christ" (Eph. 4:12). From 1 Cor. 12, notice these facts about the church: the church is the body of Christ (v. 12); the church is made up of many members (vv. 14-16); every member of the church is important and necessary (vv. 17-22). Notice further, from Eph. 4, that the body of Christ functions properly when every part does its share (v. 16). Wise elders will help the members to discover and use their talents and abilities to help the "body grow so that it builds itself up in love" (v. 16). Therefore, a wide variety of ministry opportunities should be provided in order that the members may find the areas for which they are best suited to serve. It should be remembered that in Jesus' story of the talents (Matt. 25:14-30), everyone had some gift, and each one was charged with the need to use what he had. Paul noted that each member of Christ's body has abilities from God, but "the members do not all have the same function" (Rom. 12:4). No one should be made to feel inferior because he has one gift rather than another. The important issue is that each one discovers and uses his gift (Rom. 12:6).

9. The work of elders as seen in their communication with the church.

In traveling among the churches of Christ from Maine to California, from Florida to Alaska, from Canada to England, from Italy to Israel, and from Russia to the Ukraine, the number one issue I hear between members of the church and their leaders is the lack of communication. Elders should keep the church informed in regard to what is happening. Obviously, there may be certain confidential things which elders must deal with, but the congregation needs to know what is happening in the church. Some elders have periodic "all-church" meetings which are designed as informative meetings. Whatever method is used, if elders wish for the church to be happy, confident, and united, let them communicate openly with the congregation.

10. The work of the elders as seen in conflict resolution.

The church is made up of people, and people sometimes have conflicts. How conflicts are handled is important to the life of the church. Unresolved conflict can destroy the unity of the church, and a church divided will be ineffective in its work. How should elders handle conflict? The Lord gave us two directives concerning conflict and placed responsibility upon both sides involved to correct it (Matt. 18:15-18; 5:23-24). Here are some observations based upon these two passages: The conflict must be serious because, if it is unresolved, it must be taken before the church. Those involved in conflict might be better served to "forgive and forget." Conflict affects our worship to God; therefore, it must be resolved. Elders can get the parties involved together and give guidance and direction in reaching resolution. When conflicts arise in matters of faith, the Bible is always the last word. In matters of opinions and expediency, the elders will ultimately decide. Here are some passages that will prove helpful in conflict resolution: Rom. 12:18; Phil. 2:3; 1 Cor. 12:4-7; 1 Pet. 4:11; 1 Cor. 10:23; 2 Tim. 2:22-24; Jas. 3:17.

The responsibilities of elders are great, and the judgment upon elders is sobering. The task must never be taken lightly. As members of a congregation, we also have responsibilities to the elders. The congregation is to respect, follow, obey, and submit to the elders so that their work can be done with joy (Heb. 13:17).

To serve as an elder is honorable, but it is much more than just an honorary position. It is a service of love. Those who serve well as elders have this promise from God, "When the chief Shepherd appears, you will receive the unfading crown of glory" (1 Pet. 5:4). When both elders and the congregation fulfill their God-given responsibilities, the church can effectively reach and serve souls in this lost and sinful world.

5

THINGS ELDERS DO THAT PEOPLE SEE

Ray Bowman

One of my fellow elders and I regularly visit members of the congregation in their home. It is not our purpose to try to ambush these members. We schedule our visits with the members well in advance to make sure they are not inconvenienced by it. On one such occasion, a young couple welcomed us into their home. It was a very pleasant visit with these faithful young Christians who were just starting their family. During the conversation, the young mom revealed that she had been talking to her mother that afternoon and had excused herself to finish some straightening and cleaning because she was expecting a visit from the elders. Her horrified mother responded "What have you done!?"

Far too often, that's the perception church-goers have of the eldership. They are seen as a group of men who mostly meet behind closed doors to make decisions about the business of the congregation. When they do emerge and request a meeting, there is obviously a problem. The real problem is that this image exists.

Glenn Colley explains that there are two types of elders: board room elders and living room elders. The board room elders hold meetings, make decisions, and direct the deacons in their work while making an effort to maintain a low profile. Their motives are likely pure because in many cases, they just don't want to call attention to themselves, fearing their flock might get the wrong idea that they are seeking the praise of the congregation for their work. They are mindful of Jesus' warning to "Beware of practicing your righteousness before other people in order to be seen by them, for then you will have no reward from your Father who is in heaven" (Matt. 6:1). However, I trust that none of these good men are guilty of this kind of self-aggrandizing piousness. They seek to "abstain from all appearance of evil" (1 Thess. 5:22 KJV) as they diligently, but sometimes quietly, serve their congregation.

One positive trend we can adopt from contemporary culture is the desire to be transparent. While our fellow Christians can't be privy to all the discussions and decisions of their servant-leaders, they do need to understand the direction in which the congregation is heading and how the elders are looking out for their spiritual needs.

Living room elders strive to grow and nurture personal relationships with the families they shepherd. This effort leads to the development of trust and an atmosphere of mutual love and respect that promotes a more open and transparent relationship between the elders and the members of the congregation. How do we make sure we're transparent, and the membership sees us doing what elders should do?

Show Up

Bruce Vincent is a third generation logger and motivational speaker from Libby, Montana. I met him at an agriculture conference we were both speaking at in Texas, and he fully captured the attention of the audience with one simple statement. Vincent said, "The world is run by people who show up." It doesn't always take special talents and abilities to accomplish a goal. Sometimes, it just takes being there.

One of the key themes Paul outlines in his epistles to Titus and

Timothy is that an elder needs to be an example. He doesn't say it in so many words, but when he talks about the qualities of men that should be considered, many of those things are very visible and tangible as well as spiritual. We read of the qualifications of elders in Titus and 1 Timothy. How can the congregation be sure an elder measures up to these standards set forth in Scripture? They have to see those qualities in his actions. Everybody knows those guys that are at the building "every time the doors are open." Sometimes work, travel, or other responsibilities get in the way, but an elder should make every attempt to be at worship service every time he possibly can. It's certainly one of the most notable instances of leading by example.

A good friend of mine is the president of a large corporation. He is also a faithful Christian, but he is called upon to be out of town frequently. When he is working in other areas of the country, he seeks out congregations to visit to ensure that he is "not neglecting to meet together, as is the habit of some, but encouraging one another, and all the more as you see the Day drawing near" (Heb. 10:25). He has been asked before to serve as an elder, but to his credit he declined citing the nature of his work. His decision was not an easy one, but he knew very clearly the optics dictate that an elder be available and accessible, and he was not capable of fulfilling that requirement.

When I began to serve in this capacity, a fellow elder and I decided that, to be accessible, we should hold open hours at the building at a set time every week. The theory was that anyone who had concerns could bring them to us. We even offered coffee and cookies to help seal the deal. Several weeks went by, and we had no takers, save a couple of good-hearted deacons who didn't want us to be lonely. Everyone else stayed away in droves. The lesson we learned was: if they don't come to you—you have to go to them. That's when we started scheduling home visits. Some members have politely turned down our request to visit, but the overwhelming majority welcomed us, and most even expressed a genuine appreciation for us taking the time and making the effort to come see them.

Not only can you visit the members, but you can also invite them to come to your home. That's another part of that hospitality thing that Paul talks about. Most years, Stephenia and I host a fall cookout and hayride at the farm for the congregation. We're about a half hour or more from town on some very winding roads, but even so, half or more of the membership show up even if the weather is less than perfect. Another elder holds an open house at his home during the winter holidays. Fortunately, he has a large house that accommodates a steady flow of fellowship. We have decided to host events like this rather than invite individual families to avoid the inevitable perceptions of cliquishness.

Youth rallies and events should be high on an elder's list of priorities as well. Quietly showing up and observing—and participating when invited—goes a long way towards conveying the message that you care about the future of the congregation and the lives of these young Christians. Christian families who are striving to raise believing, worshipping offspring deserve the highest recognition and support.

Paul mentions that an elder should be "able to teach." It is a good thing if an elder can stand before a group of people and conduct a lesson or preach a sermon. However, conducting Bible studies and individually leading a soul to Christ fills that obligation just as well. The congregation may not see you do the study, but they should certainly see the fruits of it.

How about potlucks and social get-togethers? Be there. Have you ever seen a politician work a room? They are trying to personalize their presence by individual interaction. Where politicians simulate a relationship by "glad-handing," elders build and reinforce relationships by genuine demonstrations of friendship, care, and concern. An elder can make a great impact in his service of the church by building relationships with the members just by showing up anytime there is an opportunity.

Show Attentiveness

Our congregation conducted a survey of the membership last year, and the results were very enlightening. Even though more than 80% of those responding gave the elders and the preacher good marks, 10% or so had no opinion, and the remainder felt we could do better. Some felt we could do a lot better and since the responses were anonymous, they saw the need to point out in very specific ways just what was wrong.

It wasn't easy to read those comments, but it was very profitable. For the most part, the criticism was that we just weren't paying attention. Many church surveys indicate the same thing; leadership is not communicating. We often take the lack of communication criticism to mean we're just not telling them enough about what's going on—there's that transparency thing again. What we might be missing is that their voices need to be heard. Communication is a two-way street, requiring the dissemination of information and the receipt of a response.

Do the members see the elders paying attention?

Show Emotion

I have a confession to make: I cry at funerals. And births. And weddings. It's not that I want to cry; it just seems like something I have little control over. The emotion builds up, and before I know it, it's running out of my eyes. For that reason, I'm seldom called upon to officiate at funerals, but that's okay because not every elder has as much trouble managing the water works as I do.

Stoicism, especially at these very emotional times, is known as a guy thing, and there's nothing wrong with controlling your feelings. I hope there's nothing wrong with being unable to, either! The problem would rest in being someone who does not have those feelings. I've known men who took great pride in boasting that "nothing bothers me." If you are an elder, or think you might be afforded the honor of serving in that capacity, I hope you've never said anything like that.

As you stand beside the casket with your arm around a grieving brother or allowing a bereaved sister to weep out her blinding tears on your shoulder, I pray that you are filled with love and compassion. Remember, at least once that we're told about, Jesus cried at a funeral, too.

> When Jesus saw her weeping, and the Jews who had come with her also weeping, he was deeply moved in his spirit and greatly troubled. And he said, "Where have you laid him?" They said to him, "Lord, come and see." Jesus wept. So the Jews said, "See how he loved him!"
>
> — John 11:33-36

This account is just one of many times we see our Lord filled with compassion. It's only reasonable to think of the man who was willing to carry the weight of the world's sin on his shoulders as being affected by physical and emotional suffering and sorrow. Compassion is defined as "a feeling of deep sympathy and sorrow for another who is stricken by misfortune, accompanied by a strong desire to alleviate the suffering." Doesn't that sound a lot like Jesus? Shouldn't that be the way a congregation sees its elders?

The waiting room at the maternity ward is a pretty emotional place, too, although for an entirely different reason. Just as tears of sadness fall as a dear soul leaves this world, tears of joy flow freely as a precious new life is welcomed into it. Being with a family at the birth of a child is one of the most enjoyable duties an elder can have. They appreciate you being with them to share their joy. However, it becomes even more important if—God forbid—something goes wrong.

Whatever the case, don't you, as an elder, want to be there? It may not be expected, but in almost every case it is appreciated.

Show Humility

I guess that sounds like an oxymoron: show humility. Being humble usually means nobody notices. However, if you truly treat others with higher regard than yourself, it really won't matter—especially to you—that your actions go unrecognized. C. S. Lewis wrote, "True humility is not thinking less of yourself; it is thinking of yourself less."

Time and time again, the Bible warns man "not to think of himself more highly than he ought to think, but to think with sober judgment, each according to the measure of faith that God has assigned" (Rom. 12:3). Do you think this is something that's of particular importance to God? I do. James devotes the entire fourth chapter of his epistle to the things that separate us from God, and then he ties all of them to the struggles Christians have with humility. "Humble yourselves before the Lord, and he will exalt you" (Jas. 4:10).

When we are awarded the mantle of responsibility that is eldership, the challenge becomes even greater as we struggle to separate our earthly desires from the will of God. In Philippians, we are told to "Do nothing from selfish ambition or conceit, but in humility count others more significant than yourselves. Let each of you look not only to his own interests, but also to the interests of others" (Phil. 2:3-4). Most people appreciate being shown they are appreciated, and elders are no different. The difficult task is to remember that what is done for the kingdom warrants no praise or reward here on earth. When appreciation is shown, we should kindly and graciously give God the glory and move on, not giving our involvement in the matter a second thought.

Show Integrity

Many elders are afforded the opportunity to serve while still actively engaged in their chosen worldly profession. As we go about our daily tasks, we should constantly be aware of the image we present to the world and, especially, to our congregation. We don't have the luxury of going home after a worship service or a business meeting and taking off our "elder suit." Those outside the body who interact with us should recognize something different about us. They should see our lives striving to grow in the qualities of 2 Peter:

> For this very reason, make every effort to supplement your faith with virtue, and virtue with knowledge, and knowledge with self-control, and self-control with steadfastness, and steadfastness with godliness, and godliness with brotherly affection, and brotherly affection with love. For if these qualities are yours and are increasing, they keep you from being ineffective or unfruitful in the knowledge of our Lord Jesus Christ.
> — 2 Pet. 1:5-8

Show Knowledge & Wisdom

Knowledge and wisdom aren't the same things, but a good elder demonstrates both. Knowledge is defined as "information, understanding, or skill that you get from experience or education." Wisdom, however, is "knowledge of what is proper or reasonable: good sense or judgment." Elders need to demonstrate knowledge of God's Word. "Do your best to present yourself to God as one approved, a worker who has no need to be ashamed, rightly handling the word of truth" (2 Tim. 2:15).

Then, wisdom comes from study and understanding and the

guidance of God through the Holy Spirit. "For where jealousy and selfish ambition exist, there will be disorder and every vile practice. But the wisdom from above is first pure, then peaceable, gentle, open to reason, full of mercy and good fruits, impartial and sincere. And a harvest of righteousness is sown in peace by those who make peace" (Jas. 3:16-18).

Sending his apostles out into the world, Jesus underscored the necessity of wisdom tempered with compassion. He told them, "Behold, I am sending you out as sheep in the midst of wolves, so be wise as serpents and innocent as doves" (Matt. 10:16). As elders, we must always seek to increase our knowledge and wisdom to be better equipped to serve our congregations.

Show Courage

Christians are courageous. Elders need to be fearless. In Deut. 31:7, Moses hands the mantle of leadership over to Joshua in a public ceremony before the Israelites, admonishing him to be "strong and courageous" in leading God's people into the Promised Land. He goes on to assure Joshua, "It is the LORD who goes before you. He will be with you; he will not leave you or forsake you. Do not fear or be dismayed" (31:8). Joshua is challenged to be courageous, but he is promised help from the Lord to meet that challenge.

In the first chapter of Joshua, God himself reaffirms the commitment Moses made, telling the new leader of the Israelites to not depart from his law, "but you shall meditate on it day and night, so that you may be careful to do according to all that is written in it. For then you will make your way prosperous, and then you will have good success. Have I not commanded you? Be strong and courageous. Do not be frightened, and do not be dismayed, for the LORD your God is with you wherever you go" (Josh. 1:8-9). God reassures his people that he will help them accomplish the tasks that he has set before them. The Israelites themselves echo God's admonition to Joshua, saying, "All that you have commanded us we will do, and wherever you send us we will go" (1:16). When we trust in God's promises, we can be equipped with the strength and courage to face the battles before us.

God supports faithful leadership, and for people to continue to remain true to God, they need an example. The church faces potential persecution on several fronts. It's not going to be easy. Twenty-first-century church leadership must encourage first-century commitment. Consider the persecution Christians faced in the first century, and yet they were assured:

> Who shall separate us from the love of Christ? Shall tribulation, or distress, or persecution, or famine, or nakedness, or danger, or sword? As it is written, "For your sake we are being killed all the day long; we are regarded as sheep to be slaughtered." No, in all these things we are more than conquerors through him who loved us. For I am sure that neither death nor life, nor angels nor rulers, nor things present nor things to come, nor powers, nor height nor depth, nor anything else in all creation, will be able to separate us from the love of God in Christ Jesus our Lord.
>
> — Rom. 8:35-39

Thomas "Stonewall" Jackson was a great leader during the War Between the States. His courage stemmed from an unshakable belief that, whatever the circumstances, God would always be in control and his will would—and should—be done. "My religious belief teaches me to feel as safe in battle as in bed. God has fixed the time for my death. I do not concern myself about that, but to be always ready, no matter when it may overtake me. ... That is the way all men should live, and then all would be equally brave." As elders, it is possible (though highly unlikely) that our role will put us in a life or death situation. However, if we can face any and all challenges with the faith that Jackson articulated, why would we even momentarily hesitate to do what God's Word tells us is right?

Our courage, appropriately displayed before our congregations, will empower and embolden them to put aside their fears and embrace the promise of the apostle Paul in Rom. 8:31, "What then shall we say to these things? If God is for us, who can be against us?"

When your congregation looks at you, what do they see?

6

THINGS ELDERS DO THAT PEOPLE DON'T SEE

Steve Bailey

An elder is to be many things to many people, but most importantly, he is to serve God. It seems that elders have the wonderful task placed before them to fill many shoes, or wear many different hats, all of which fall under the biblical title of a shepherd. It has been my honor to be an elder for eight years at the time of this writing. I've been preaching for forty years. Many have gone before me who have served much longer as an elder. Hundreds could write a much better chapter on what it means to be an elder and how to serve in the Lord's church. Nonetheless, I will hopefully add something to the discussion of what an elder does in his role of leadership in the greatest institution in the world.

My service as an elder has the added benefit of serving as both a gospel preacher and an elder at the same time. Many believe this is the double honor spoken by Paul in 1 Tim. 5:17, "Let the elders who rule well be considered worthy of double honor, especially those who labor in preaching and teaching." We know also that Peter was both an elder and a preacher by his own words recorded in 1 Pet. 5:1-5,

> So I exhort the elders among you, as a fellow elder and a witness of the sufferings of Christ, as well as a partaker in the glory that is going to be revealed:

> shepherd the flock of God that is among you, exercising oversight, not under compulsion, but willingly, as God would have you; not for shameful gain, but eagerly; not domineering over those in your charge, but being examples to the flock. And when the chief Shepherd appears, you will receive the unfading crown of glory. Likewise, you who are younger, be subject to the elders. Clothe yourselves, all of you, with humility toward one another, for "God opposes the proud but gives grace to the humble."

There is a great deal of honor and praise in these verses, but serving as an elder in the Lord's church is also humbling. We must recognize that a great deal of dedication and work goes into this "double" ministry.

Preachers have the opportunity to know a great deal about the membership through the different roads of ministry. People make appointments to sit down and visit regarding various topics of discussion, many of which have to do with personal issues. These may include issues of sin, grief, frustrations over personal matters, guilt resulting from sin in their lives, and some of the most difficult family matters. These issues weigh heavily on the mind of a Christian. Often, they need their shepherds to talk with, to pray with, and to ask God's help in releasing some burden or to petition God for a clearer answer.

The minister can help in these areas, but an elder also helps by serving in confidence. In doing so, the elder gives assurance that God knows their pain and the assurance that God gives in removing the guilt that weighs many down in this hard world. Fellow elders can pray privately and collectively for these individuals. Elders have "an ear to the ground" on behalf of the flock. When a sheep goes wandering off the path, the shepherd needs to bring them back to the fold of safety. Elders do that with a great deal of love, concern, and sometimes even confrontation. The ministry of a shepherd is not always the "easy life!" When good things happen at a congregation, people often say sweet and complimentary words about the congregation. When things don't go as smoothly as they could or once did, the elders, often undeservedly and very quickly, get the blame.

The New Testament uses the imagery of a shepherd to help us understand more about being an elder. Growing up in West Texas, I was around sheep from time to time. You can't live in Texas and not see sheep in the pasture or being brought to livestock sales. I do not know everything about sheep, but quite honestly, they are not very smart. Sheep will frighten easily. When sheep are walking a path, they will usually follow one after another. It is like they are playing "follow the leader" as they follow the path. If the lead sheep jumps into the air or leaps in fright over something real or imagined, all of the following sheep will have the same reaction. They may not even know the reason they are leaping, but they leap anyway! However, if the lead sheep is calm, the sheep following will all be calm. A shepherd reassures his flock with his own sense of calmness and reassurance. When the flock knows the shepherd is protecting and watching out for grievous wolves in the world, they feel calm and safe.

The techniques of raising healthy sheep, herding sheep, and growing a flock are basically the same since the time of creation. Generally speaking, sheep have bad eye sight, get sick easily, and wander from the fold of safety. Sheep need fresh, still water to drink, and they need good pasture land in which to eat clean, fresh grass. Perhaps all of this is why God calls His children "sheep, " and set forth shepherds to help guide us. Elders are to help the members of the body of Christ to have these same things in a spiritual sense.

Elders are to spiritually protect the flock. They are charged with the great task of making sure what is taught from the pulpit, in the class room, and to the youth of our congregation is sound biblical teaching. Elders are to insure it is the pure Word of God; biblical and beneficial to the flock so they may be nourished with a proper diet of God's Word.

Elders are to refresh the flock from time to time with some added nutrients to the diet. A good dose of missions should be added as a bonus to the diet of a congregation. Missions help the flock to see the wider picture of global soul-saving. It is important to remind the congregation that we are charged with a great commission to take the saving message of Christ to the entire world. Inviting a special speaker two or three times a year encourages continued mission work. The Mesquite congregation spends an entire month emphasizing the work of missions and how we can help take the message of Christ to a lost world. We end the month with a special contribution dedicated totally to our mission points.

Traveling abroad and actually visiting a supported mission site with some of the membership instills a heart for missions. It allows members to have a hands-on experience of mission work. These visits now become a place they have actually seen with their own eyes, and not just a place talked about in reports. This gives the congregation a vision with greater understanding of global missions.

Weekend workshops and special seminars are always a delightful way to add to the spiritual diet of the membership. Classes and seminars over a variety of topics are beneficial for a congregation. These sessions can focus on a particular book of the Bible, singing, worship, outreach or the family. Revivals and gospel meetings seem to be a thing of the past in many congregations, but elders have the charge to "feed the flock" in whatever way they determine to be best and most beneficial.

Various media resources can certainly be an added bonus we can use in sharing the message of Christ today. The full use of the Internet has not been explored completely. One inexpensive way to teach is through the medium of Skype. This is a great way to "electronically visit" mission sites and encourage preachers in the mission field. Facebook, Twitter, mass emails, and social media all have their place in this modern time. Elders have so many ways to equip their members and get the message out to the world!

Elders' workshops and retreats provide a wonderful venue to hear other elders explain how they deal with issues. Of course, great care is taken to conduct these events in a manner of strict confidence by withholding names of individuals in situations that may be discussed. Elders can pull from experiences of one congregation to help another. God has created each congregation to be autonomous, but that does not prohibit elderships from helping others in matters of experience or advice sharing.

Elders have many tasks, and serving as a shepherd is not always easy. As the old saying goes, "If it was easy, everyone would be doing it!" The good times always outweigh the bad in serving in the eldership. But when things are tough…they are really tough! The members need to pray daily for the elders and tell their elders how much they are appreciated. For many elders, the last time they were told a word of appreciation was the day they were ordained as an elder. Brethren, this should not be! Mention your elders by name when praying in the public assembly and in private prayers. God will bless them and encourage them in the great ministry and work that has been placed before them.

What do elders do? Many, many things. Do they do them all perfectly? Of course not; they are human. But always remember, elders do try to do their best in serving God. The membership can help the elders to serve God and his church by supporting them and expressing words of encouragement to them. The Hebrew writer said in Heb. 13:17, "Obey your leaders and submit to them, for they are keeping watch over your souls, as those who will have to give an account. Let them do this with joy and not with groaning, for that would be of no advantage to you."

In the remainder of this chapter I have used alliteration to highlight some of the unseen things elders do in the work of the local congregation.

Faith

God expects elders to help the flock with the formation of faith, growing the faith of individual members, and strengthening the faith that is necessary to persevere in a world that is only our temporary home. Each Christian needs to know that we are in this world for a short period of time. James reminds us in Jas. 4:14, "Yet you do not know what tomorrow will bring. What is your life? For you are a mist that appears for a little time and then vanishes."

Formation of faith begins with the birth of a baby and continues to the grave. Cradle roll classes are essential to help accentuate what the parents are doing at home to help shape a child's faith. The church must not be perceived as the only exposure to the Bible and its truths, but it should serve to assist the family in study and growth. The parents must be the first line of instruction! The church can help greatly with a well-balanced curriculum that teaches the Bible from Genesis through Revelation over the years the students attend classes. The formation of faith is vital, and elders have a responsibility to help with this. In past years, many congregations hired a minister of education to insure continuity of study and growth for all ages. Unfortunately, the hiring of education ministers has fallen off the radar with other expenses taking its place. A poor education curriculum could result in a decline of over all knowledge of God's Word that leads to a decline in membership. Faith is imparted through study and growth in God's Word to see his wonderful promises carried out in Scripture, which leads to a building of faith for tomorrow.

The Hebrews writer instructs us: "Now faith is the assurance of things hoped for, the conviction of things not seen" (11:1). The church must have faith for today that will carry her members throughout the future. We must all build a faith that will carry us to the great reward of heaven.

Fellowship

Another essential thing that elders try their best to instill in the local congregation is the sweet fellowship of the body of Christ. The time spent with the brethren is key to knowing the flock individually and as a group. One of the requirements of a shepherd is to be hospitable. Paul told Timothy this in 1 Tim. 3:2, "An overseer must be … hospitable." When an elder and his wife recognize the importance of being hospitable, they serve the congregation well. They open their home to members and have one-on-one meetings with families as they extend themselves to the fellowship of the body of Christ.

Planned fellowships for the local congregations are usually a hit with the members. As a boy, I remember the church using the National Guard Armory as a place of fellowship. Many men in the congregation were hunters, and the barbecue venison dinner was an annual event. The singing and fellowship that took place at those dinners is a wonderful memory. Fourth of July or New Year's Eve singings are still held in many congregations, and annual holiday gatherings are conducted with great anticipation. All of these events add to the fact that members need each other, and that is evident at these functions.

Area-wide gatherings are so important to the life and fellowship of the local congregation. Cities with multiple congregations need the experience of worshipping together from time to time. This demonstrates to the community that the congregations love one another and enjoy each other's company. In places where there are issues that separate congregations, those issues need to be worked on by the elderships in a way that can promote fellowship when at all possible. People need to learn that if we are going to be in heaven together, we need to get along here on earth.

Finance

As most people realize, it takes money to do just about anything in our day. The work of the church is no exception. Elders make it possible to challenge the membership with great works and ministries. To accomplish these goals, it must be explained very clearly that to carry out the plans, it requires money and proper budgeting. When the church is challenged, the brethren usually come through for the things they believe in.

I am reminded about an eldership who took on a very well thought out and costly building expansion. The spokesman for the eldership took the podium and said, "We want everyone to relax this morning—the money for the building expansion has been found!" The members were all so happy with smiles of joy on their faces. The elder then said, "The problem, however, is that the money is in your pockets!" Yes, it takes money to do many things in the church today. I do not know who said it, but I remember a preacher saying, "The gospel message is free…it is free for everyone! But just like the water that is piped into our homes and businesses, we have to pay to get the water from one point to another, and the plumbing is costly!" God wants all men to come to repentance; his desire is for no one to be lost. We must get the message of the gospel out to a dying world. The bottom line is this: it takes money to go across the street and across the ocean!

Can you think of one thing that screams excellence more than being a good steward and giving to God? Elders have a wonderful task of teaching stewardship to the membership. Most of us have heard the old adage that 20% of the members do 80% of the work. It may be just as accurate to say that 20% of the members are doing the "heavy lifting" when it comes to consistent giving in the church.

The church can do anything that God blesses, and the doors of opportunity will open wide to his efforts. All the church needs today are the funds to do the greatest work on earth. Elders, let's encourage our membership to meet that challenge with a well thought out spending plan that will glorify God.

Fights

This topic may seem strange, but keeping with the pattern of words that begin with "F," I thought about elders dealing with strife or brethren who are fighting in the local church. I once heard of an eldership that was not getting along. One night in a meeting, voices were raised, a fist was pounded on the table more than once, and one of the older men said, "Gentlemen, I think we need to all stop right now and pray about this!" One of the younger men said in an off-stage whisper, "Oh no! Has it really come to that?" Elders may disagree at times, and maybe there is room for disagreement and a strong argument made on both sides of the topic, but it is never helpful to fight with one another.

Likewise, members should not be involved in strong disagreements. Paul gives an indication that two women were not getting along in the church in Philippi. In Phil. 4:2-3 we read, "I entreat Euodia and I entreat Syntyche to agree in the Lord. Yes, I ask you also, true companion, help these women, who have labored side by side with me in the gospel together with Clement and the rest of my fellow workers, whose names are in the book of life." It appears that Euodia and Syntyche were involved in some disagreement, and it was so evident that others knew about it, and Paul had to address the topic.

When disturbances take place between brothers and/or sisters, it may be necessary for elders to request a meeting of the individual parties and help resolve the issue(s). When giving counsel to such matters, it is essential to pray about that meeting before hand and come to the meeting with listening ears. Most issues can be resolved with a good clear discussion, patience, and love. But if these issues are left alone to fester and grow, only more heartache and anger will come. Elders are to help keep peace in the church.

Fruit-Bearing

Many congregations have seen revivals and gospel meeting dates dwindle from two-week-long meetings to one-week meetings, and now many congregations have only week-end efforts or a one-day Sunday event. The busy lives of the brethren have taken a toll on many evangelistic efforts. Unfortunately, this has made it necessary to take a long and hard look at the fact that the brethren in many places will no longer support gospel meetings or revivals. Congregations have reaped the seeds sown of low attendance and half-hearted attendance to the extent that many congregations have abandoned this type of gathering. Along with that decision, evangelism is on the decline, and elders are on the constant search for methods and ways to equip and encourage members to reach out to the lost.

If elders asked their members if they really want to see the local congregation grow, the answer would be 100% in the affirmative. But many times, the proof is in the attendance by the members when opportunities are given to reach out and evangelize the community. When I was a younger man, our congregation was having a gospel meeting, and one man was asked if he would lead prayer on Tuesday night of the meeting. He responded by saying, "Sorry, Tuesday nights are my bowling night!" With dedication levels like that, it is no surprise we have seen the decline of support for our evangelistic efforts.

Elders must realize that families are very busy raising their children today. Let's face it; families today are pulled in many directions. To say that all young families have their priorities out of place only adds to the guilt many single mothers and fathers already have in the brief time they have with their children. Placing guilt or shame on members does not and will not work. Some of those family units will simply vote with their feet and leave the congregation for another.

Perhaps one way of encouraging the modern family is to give the members dates of major events a year in advance. This will help busy families mark and arrange their calendars. We should not blame members for going on vacations when their company requires them to submit dates for leave nine to ten months in advance. When the church does not plan events well, we will continue to get what we have always gotten: poor attendance. A well planned office staff helps the congregation. A popular way of sharing this information is to mail "Save the Date" invitations. These cards can be mass mailed, electronically delivered via church email, Facebook, or Twitter accounts and will help the members plan.

Jesus Christ left us with the Great Commission. Mark 16:15-16 commands us: "Go into all the world and proclaim the gospel to the whole creation. Whoever believes and is baptized will be saved, but whoever does not believe will be condemned." Members of the body know these verses well. Most struggle with how to do it! As elders, let's help our congregation take the gospel to the lost by praying, planning, and leading by example.

When I was a younger minster, I remember very well an older minister taking me on a Bible study. I was so happy when the study concluded with the person being baptized. It was a wise man who invited me to go along with him that day. I have tried to share that same goal with younger men over the years. Taking a young man on a visit to the hospital, or to visit a spiritually weak member, or to visit a shut-in that needs a prayer and a smile could help that young person develop a love for service in the church. You never know— you might be training a young man for the eldership someday.

Finality of Life

I have conducted my share of funerals over the years. They are never easy, and often are difficult. An elder truly serves the church when he prepares the congregation for the finality of life. The old saying is so true, "None of us are getting out of this world alive!" Of course, we know that the Lord will return someday, and if we are alive, we will not face death but be taken up with him. Many have already gone on to their reward and many will still pass from this life. We must be prepared spiritually, mentally, and even financially for death.

How many members have a will prepared? Is the church mentioned in the will? After the death of a person, it is often difficult for funds to be dispersed to the local church. Financial matters must be talked about while one is living and made clear to other family members. This is part of being a good steward.

Spiritually speaking, we have the task of preparing our membership for the judgment. Bible classes, sermons, workshops, outreach efforts and engaging one's talent(s) in the kingdom are so vital to the preparation of going home to be with God. Most members ask, "What is my talent?" Some members struggle all their life asking what they can really do well in the church. As elders we can help to engage and equip members to find their talent and use that talent for God. The best way I have found to discover a person's talent is to simply ask, "What do you like to do?" And then answer with, "We have a ministry for you, will you take it on? If the church budget will help with funds for the ministry, even help you with some guidelines and purpose of the ministry, will you take this work as your ministry of service?" Many people are waiting to be asked. As elders, we cannot allow the 20% to do all of the work of the church. The 20% will soon wear out, and the 80% will ask, "Why didn't you call me and ask me to help!"

Elders have an awesome responsibility to carry on the work of the Lord in the local congregation. It is with great thanks and appreciation that God in his wisdom planned for a plurality of elders in the local congregation. Simply said, this work is too much for one man. God knew that there is strength in numbers to lead his church. May God help us to lead the family of God in faith, fellowship, finance, fights, fruit bearing, and finality of life.

7

TRAINING YOUNG MEN TO BE LEADERS

Howard Norton

By the grace of God, I am an elder of the Lord's church. This is my fourth time to be approached about serving in this role, the third time I have accepted, and the second congregation where I have been one of the shepherds. It is a pleasure and an honor to serve the Lord Jesus Christ in this way. I believe my fellow overseers and I have been appointed by the Holy Spirit to shepherd this local flock, and we take the task seriously.

Finding men to serve as elders is often difficult. First, it is difficult because many lack the biblical qualifications they must possess in order to do the job. These qualifications are mentioned in passages such as 1 Tim. 3, Tit. 1, and 1 Pet. 5. Second, men who do meet these requirements often appear to have no desire to accept the appointment. They do not aspire to the job and, therefore, lack a fundamental ingredient for functioning as a shepherd of the flock. According to the Bible, "If anyone aspires to the office of overseer, he desires a noble task" (1 Tim. 3:1). We understand that the desire to serve is an important qualification since Peter adds that the elder should exercise "oversight, not under compulsion, but willingly, as God would have you" (1 Pet. 5:3).

In training young men to be elders, we need to provide the

spiritual nurturing for youth that accomplishes two vital tasks: (1) leads them to desire the office of an overseer and (2) produces the spiritual formation that elders must have in order to serve. My purpose in this chapter is to give suggestions as to how the church today can do this. Since I am an elder, my approach will be largely autobiographical—what God's people did for me as a young man made me want to develop the needed qualifications so that I would be able to serve as an elder. I make no claim to perfection in either area. However, I have learned that as desirable as perfection is, God's work will always have to be done by people who fall short. I am one of those imperfect shepherds who is trying to be God's man.

CREATING THE DESIRE TO SERVE

My parents came from Christian parents who came from Christian parents. I was blessed to be born to a mother and father who were committed to being servants of Christ. From my earliest days, I remember being in Sunday school and church. My uncles and aunts were also members of the Lord's church, and several uncles were preachers. My maternal grandfather had been a preacher before his death when I was still a child, and my paternal grandfather was a well-known song leader in the Fort Worth, TX area. I was always at home in church even though I squirmed, fidgeted, misbehaved, and then faced the consequences when we returned to the house.

As I grew older, the children at church became my playmates before and after services. Later on, these children became adolescents who were my friends. Still later on, the girls became my girlfriends, and the guys became my buddies. We were a kind of Christian gang. I couldn't wait to arrive at church on Sunday morning, Sunday night, and Wednesday night, and any other times possible between those days. I loved to go to church and be with my age group; that meant more to me than words can ever express.

I determined early on that I wanted to be a preacher when I grew up. I had no idea how I would earn money to support a family, but I knew I wanted to preach and serve God. As a boy, I was confident that I could make a living during the week and preach and teach in the local church without worrying about money and without expecting any financial support from the brethren. Although a little naïve, I still believe that this is the spirit a real preacher needs to have if he wants to serve God faithfully as a minister of the word. Money will not be the primary consideration for one who feels the Lord wants him to preach.

My two uncles, J. Willard and J. Bennett Morrow, preached at the Rosen Heights Church of Christ in Fort Worth where my family and I attended. They both had a deep commitment to developing young men into preachers and church leaders. To do that, they conducted a one-hour Young People's Class every Sunday just before the evening worship. This program was based on the theory that people "learn to do by doing." It was not a Bible study but rather a class where young people practiced doing what the adults did in the regular worship. Boys would direct songs, lead prayers, read Scriptures, recite memory work, preach a sermonette, and make announcements. Girls would recite poetry and Bible memory work. Sometimes, boys and girls would sing a special children's song. This training program took place every Sunday night year round. What made it work was the presence of the parents and other members who wanted to encourage young people to serve God.

I preached my first sermon in the Young People's Class when I was about nine years old. Mother prepared it, and it was entitled "Blessed Are the Peacemakers." She used the story of Abraham and Lot to illustrate how Abraham desired peace with Lot more than he desired the choice part of the land because the two were family. It was a wonderful little sermon that has helped shape my life. All I had to do was read what Mother wrote, but I got my feet wet and discovered

I could actually stand before an audience and speak. From that point on, there was no turning back.

In a different but similar class, my Uncle Willard was training a group of us junior high school kids and announced one day that I was going to preach the imaginary funeral of a man who had died. I stumbled through the experience. It was my first attempt at doing a funeral. After that, he would often ask me to read a Scripture at funeral services he conducted. Some years later, just after moving to my first full-time preaching position, I answered a knock at the door and found that a man in the community had died. Although not a faithful Christian, he had always said he wanted a preacher from the church of Christ to do his funeral. I was that man, and I was about to do my very first official funeral. I didn't learn to do a funeral in college; I learned to do a funeral in that training class and by participating in funeral services my uncle conducted. I was grateful to God for helping me make it through my first funeral without disgracing the local church, the Lord, or myself, and I was grateful to the Rosen Heights church and my Uncle Willard for teaching me how to do it.

What I didn't fully realize, perhaps, was that the Young People's Class was not just training us to lead in the work of the Lord and enjoy it; it was preparing us for leadership period. Most of the young people at Rosen Heights attended J. P. Elder Junior High School. In the ninth grade, students were eligible to run for student body offices. The seventh, eighth, and ninth-graders elected these officers for the 1,200 member student body. When I was in the ninth grade, the president, vice president, secretary, and treasurer were all members of the Rosen Heights Church of Christ! The following year, the student body president was also from that small local church. How did it happen? It happened because the church trained its young people to lead and like it. They learned to do by doing.

If we want young people to become elders one day, we must equip them with the desire and ability to be leaders of men and women. Too often our young people's programs are designed to teach young people to sit in a corner and be sure not to do anything wrong. What we need are young people who are trained to do what's right and lead their classmates and friends to do the same. They need to learn at an early age to stand up for Jesus and do "whatever is true, whatever is honorable, whatever is just, whatever is pure, whatever is lovely, whatever is commendable" (Phil. 4:8). If we do this, I believe we won't have any trouble finding men who aspire to be elders in the Lord's church.

DEVELOPING QUALIFIED MEN TO SERVE

Desiring to be an elder is an important qualification for men who serve in this role, but much more than desire is required in order to be effective. In fact, the desire to serve can be a dangerous characteristic if a person does not manage it carefully. Several years ago, I assigned a paper to each of my graduate students. The paper was to be a brief history of a local church. I preferred that it be a history of the congregation where each one was serving. One student told about a congregation in which the elder selection process went bad—so bad, in fact, that partisans of one candidate to the eldership made portable signs advocating his selection and marched up and down the aisles carrying his propaganda. The desire to serve is noble when it is properly controlled and the desire is for the correct purpose. Beware of the man who desires the office for the wrong reasons!

The qualifications outlined by Paul and Peter, therefore, are critical in the appointment of elders. The focus of these qualifications is on the spiritual and emotional maturity of the individuals under consideration. Besides 1 Tim. 3, Tit. 1, and 1 Pet. 5, other passages can also help us when choosing elders. I was once in a discussion about church leadership and asked a friend what he would recommend for people to read who were thinking about becoming deacons. He surprised me when he said, "I would encourage them to read the life of Christ in the Gospel of Mark." At the time, I thought, "That has nothing to do with deacons." I was wrong. Preachers, teachers, elders, and deacons are striving to be servants, and the life of Christ has everything to do with being a servant! When a person is considering the eldership, his spiritual preparation should begin with imitating Jesus. The sooner he begins that practice, the better.

One of the most critical questions in looking for qualified men is, "Does he demonstrate the mind of Christ?" Does he, for example, look like the description of Jesus in Phil. 2—a person who counts others better than himself, who thinks about the interests of others and not just his own, who is willing to give up the rights and privileges of divine Sonship in order to come to earth as a man, live as a servant, and die as a common criminal for crimes he didn't commit?

In my opinion, one of the most powerful biblical descriptions of the work and character of an elder is Psa. 23: "The LORD is my shepherd; I shall not want. He makes me lie down in green pastures. He leads me beside still waters. He restores my soul. He leads me in paths of righteousness for his name's sake." True, King David wrote Psalm 23 some 1,000 years before the church was established; but the characteristics of a good shepherd are for all generations—especially when the shepherd is Jehovah God. When a man is thinking about becoming an elder and wants to know what qualifications are needed and what his duties will be, Psa. 23 is a good place to start. He needs to be an imitator of God our Shepherd and seek to be like him in word and deed. He needs to be willing to care for people just as God does: to keep them properly fed and nourished, to keep them safe, to provide refreshment for their souls when they are weary, and to lead the flock in paths of goodness and purity to ultimate glory and victory over our spiritual enemies.

Another insightful passage for the prospective elder to study carefully is John 10. In this passage, Jesus describes himself as the good shepherd and says, "The good shepherd lays down his life for the sheep" (John 10:11). Jesus also says the sheep recognize the shepherd's voice, and he knows them by name. He steps out front and leads the flock, and the flock follows because it trusts him to provide for its needs in the hour of trouble. A man considering his own qualifications to be a shepherd does well to study Jesus Christ and imitate his selfless love for people. Although there are many facets to the work of an elder or shepherd, the task ultimately involves working with people and gently leading them toward heaven. It is not about gaining personal power or prestige. People who seek these two benefits must be weeded out in the selection process.

With the previous passages as background, we now are ready to pay closer attention to 1 Tim. 3 and Tit. 1. Each of these chapters has a lengthy list of needed qualifications specifically for the elders/bishops/overseers/shepherds of a local church. A number of years ago, a Bible-church minister named Gene A. Getz wrote an excellent book entitled *The Measure of a Man*. He took each elder qualification in the letters to Timothy and Titus and wrote a chapter concerning its meaning in the life of a man. In Getz's opinion, the measure of a real man was to be determined by how closely he came to meeting the qualifications laid down by the Holy Spirit for elders. In other words, a man possessing the qualifications of elders as given in 1 Tim. 3 and Tit. 1 would be God's picture of the ideal man. I believe Getz had a clear insight into the qualifications needed to be a shepherd of the flock. The shepherd of the flock needs to be the very model of a real Christian man—the ideal brother in Christ.

Perhaps two of the most worrisome characteristics in these two lists for men considering the eldership are that the shepherd must "be above reproach," and he must "be able to teach." There are some other characteristics that require careful thought, but these two—especially the first one mentioned—often surface as men evaluate themselves and their qualifications to serve in the shepherding role.

What does "above reproach" mean? I know what it doesn't mean. It doesn't mean that a man has to be perfect before he can be an overseer in the Lord's church. If some man somewhere claims he is perfect and without sin, he is definitely not qualified to be an elder. In fact, according to John, "If we say we have no sin, we deceive ourselves, and the truth is not in us" (1 John 1:8). We certainly don't want that kind of man in leadership, but we do need men who are "above reproach."

In fact, all church members are to be "above reproach." The Greek word used for this elder qualification in Tit. 1 is sometimes translated "blameless, irreproachable." It is a qualification for deacons in 1 Tim. 3:10 and a quality of Christians in general in 1 Cor. 1:8 and Col. 1:22. In these latter two passages, it is clear that "above reproach" is a condition we have a right to claim only by the grace of God and is not a literal perfection or sinlessness that we have achieved on our own. We are "above reproach" because God has forgiven us of our sins through the blood of Christ, and we are constantly being cleansed by that blood as we walk in the light as He is in the light (John 1:7). If perfection were a requirement for being a shepherd or bishop, Paul and Barnabas would never have been able to appoint elders in every church, as recorded in Acts 14:23. As a matter of fact, only a man who recognizes his weaknesses is qualified to be an overseer of the flock.

As to the qualification, "able to teach," this surely doesn't mean a man must be an orator or a Bible scholar in the sense of one who has studied the Bible as a discipline of higher education for ten or twelve years. Even the apostles didn't have that length of training when they began to preach. In fact, they were considered uneducated, common men. The difference was that they had been with Jesus and were aided in their message by the Holy Spirit. We don't necessarily need the most highly educated people as elders today, although we are grateful when we have them. We need common men who know and love God's inspired word and, in the words of Paul, "hold firm to the trustworthy word as taught, so that [they] may be able to give instruction in sound doctrine and also to rebuke those who contradict it" (Tit. 1:9). Whether a man is able to do this one-on-one, in small groups, before a classroom of students, or on a podium before a multitude of listeners, he qualifies as "able to teach."

CONCLUSION

We desperately need good elders to shepherd the Lord's church. They must desire the office and meet the qualifications set forth by the Holy Spirit to occupy such an important position in God's kingdom. In order for churches in the future to enjoy the leadership that willing, qualified men can provide, our training of these leaders must begin while they are still young people. I have tried to show in this chapter that the best way to create desire in men to serve as shepherds is to train them in the work of the Lord while they are growing up in the local church. Let them learn to do by doing.

As they experience the joy of service and hear hundreds or thousands of lessons about how to live in order to please God, the invitation to serve as elders will not sound like a call to take a gigantic leap into the unknown. Becoming overseers will seem a natural step forward in their desire to serve God. What will surprise them, however, will be the fact that they reached the age of "elder" so quickly.

8

APPOINTING NEW ELDERS

Jerrie Barber

Fifty years ago in my early days of preaching, when it was time for appointing new elders, the present elders would discuss the need and the men who might serve. They would then approach the men and get their consent and tell the congregation it was time to appoint new elders. They would announce the men they had selected and give the congregation two weeks to give scriptural objections. If no objections were given, the men would begin their service after they were appointed. During those years as I was asked to study and preach sermons on church leadership and the qualifications of elders and deacons, I noticed that selecting and appointing leaders were two distinct actions. When we consider any area of service to God, we should always begin by asking, "What does the Bible say?"

Appointing Elders

The Bible tells us that Paul, Barnabas, and Titus appointed men as elders. In Acts 14:23, Paul and Barnabas "appointed elders for them in every church, with prayer and fasting they committed them to the Lord in whom they had believed." In this verse, the word *appoint* means to "to formally appoint or assign someone to a particular task—to appoint, to assign."[1]

In Tit. 1:5, Titus was instructed to appoint elders. Paul writes, "This is why I left you in Crete, so that you might put what remained into order, and appoint elders in every town as I directed you." In this verse, the word *appoint* is defined as "to assign to someone a position of authority over others—to put in charge of, to appoint, to designate."[2]

We also can read that the Holy Spirit appointed elders. In this instance, the verse uses the word *overseers* for the office of elder. Acts 20:28 says, "Therefore take heed to yourselves and to all the flock, among which the Holy Spirit has made you overseers, to shepherd the church of God which He purchased with His own blood" (NKJV). The word used for *made* in this verse is defined as "to assign someone to a particular task, function, or role—to appoint, to designate, to assign, to give a task to."[3]

So we read of both men and the Holy Spirit giving the chosen men authority to carry out the duties of an elder in different congregations by appointing them, but nothing is said in these verses about how these men were selected.

Selecting Elders

How did God's people select leaders? In the Old Testament, Moses commanded the people to choose capable men, and then he appointed the men they chose. When all of Israel was gathered "on this side of Jordan in the wilderness" (Deut. 1:1), Moses instructed them to, "'Choose for your tribes wise, understanding, and experienced men, and I will appoint them as your heads.' And you answered me, 'The thing that you have spoken is good for us to do'" (Deut. 1:13-14). In this passage, we can observe the following about the selection of leaders for Israel:

Moses said:

1. You (all Israel) choose.
2. I will make them heads over you.

The Bible also gives us a New Testament example of the church selecting men to serve. We can read about how the apostles led the church to select special servants to carry out the task of distributing food to the widows in Acts 6:1-6. The account says:

> Now in these days when the disciples were increasing in number, a complaint by the Hellenists arose against the Hebrews because their widows were being neglected in the daily distribution. And the twelve summoned the full number of the disciples and said, "It is not right that we should give up preaching the word of God to serve tables. Therefore, brothers, pick out from among you seven men of good repute, full of the Spirit and of wisdom, whom we will appoint to this duty. But we will devote ourselves to prayer and to the ministry of the word." And what they said pleased the whole gathering, and they chose Stephen, a man full of faith and of the Holy Spirit, and Philip, and Prochorus, and Nicanor, and Timon, and Parmenas, and Nicolaus, a proselyte of Antioch. These they set before the apostles, and they prayed and laid their hands on them.

In this passage, we can observe the following about the selection of the men to serve:

1. You (multitude) seek out the men.
2. We (apostles) will appoint.

3. They (multitude) chose.
4. The apostles laid hands on them.
5. The multitude selected.
6. The apostles appointed.

We've already defined the word used for *appoint* in this passage, but it will be helpful to consider the meanings of two other words that are important in this study. The term translated *seek out* means "to choose or select on the basis of having investigated carefully—to select carefully, to choose after careful investigation."[4] And the word *chose* is defined as "to make a choice of one or more possible alternatives—to choose, to select, to prefer."[5]

From my study of the Bible, when God's people recognized new leaders, the group selected, and the leaders appointed. This process promotes support of the group for the new leaders. When Moses told all Israel to choose their leaders, they told Moses, "The thing that you have spoken is good for us to do" (Deut. 1:14). When the apostles instructed the disciples to select men to be appointed over the business of feeding the widows, we learn that "what they said pleased the whole gathering" (Acts 6:5).

Objections to Members Selecting

Many elders object to letting the congregation select elders and deacons. I recall a time when I was a young preacher, and my elders were discussing adding to the leadership. They talked about whom they wanted to serve with them. As we discussed the process, I asked the question, "Have you considered letting the congregation select the men who will serve?" I had studied Acts 6 and wondered about it.

Their reply was, "If you turn all those people loose, there's no telling who they may come up with." These men were charter elders of the congregation—the first elders the congregation had ever appointed. When these elders were appointed several years before, the congregation had gone through a process, selected them, and they were ordained. However, now these men selected by the congregation didn't trust the church to have the same wisdom it had when its members selected them.

Let's consider these questions:

- Who do you believe was the best selector of people who ever lived?

- Who was the best teacher who ever lived?

- Who was the best trainer who ever lived?

My answer to all three questions is Jesus! Jesus instructed the apostles to carry on his work after his ascension. I don't think we will find a smarter, wiser, more spiritually minded leadership team than the apostles. They certainly had the ability to select good men. However, they said, "You select. We will appoint."

The Bible doesn't give a method of selecting and appointing elders and deacons. Since we don't have a direct example or command, we must look to biblical principles for guidance and make sure that the method we use does not violate any biblical principle. It is my observation that many congregations have two weeks of "legalized gossip" during the appointing of leadership. I have heard this announcement, "Here are the men we are putting before you to serve as elders if there are no objections. If anyone has a scriptural objection, he or she should write it out, sign it, and hand it to one of the elders. We will never reveal who wrote the letter."

Jesus has a better plan. He said if someone has "missed the mark," we are to go to that person alone and discuss it with him (Matt. 18:15). We should not be a talebearer about a person considering and being considered as an elder. If we believe something is wrong or lacking in that man, we should talk with him, express the good qualities we see in him, and share our concerns. Perhaps there was a misunderstanding on our part. It may be we have seen something he has not considered. Often the visit clears up doubts. If it doesn't, there is still time to bring others in to help with the disagreement. Jesus suggests that (Matt. 18:16).

Elders are often concerned about an unqualified person being selected if they don't control the entire process. That will not happen if they are involved as members. If an elder has an objection or question about any suggested individual, he has the right and obligation to talk with him about his concern and take it as far as the evidence warrants. But each elder should go to that brother as a concerned Christian and not as a group.

Should Preachers Select?

We examined the Bible accounts of Paul, Barnabas, and Titus appointing elders (Acts 14:23, Tit. 1:5). Considering these verses, should preachers, especially in new churches, select the men who are qualified to lead and shepherd?

In his book, *A Treatise on the Eldership*, J. W. McGarvey makes three observations on these accounts of initial elderships being established. First, he makes comments on the difference in selecting and ordaining:

> We have only one example on record, in which we are distinctly told what part was taken by the congregation, and what by the ordaining officers. This is the case of the seven deacons of the church in Jerusalem. The Apostles called together "the multitude of the disciples," and said, "Look you out among you seven men of honest report, full of the Holy Spirit and wisdom, whom we may appoint over this business"

(Acts 6.2– 3). The selection, then, was made by the multitude, and the appointment by the apostles.[6]

Second, he comments on Paul and Barnabas:

> Now, in the case of the elders in the churches of Lycaonia and Pisidia, it is said that Paul and Barnabas "ordained them"; or, to express it more accurately, "appointed them" (Acts 14.23). The word here rendered appoint (cheirotoneo) is not the one so rendered in Acts 6.3; but in such a connection its current meaning is about the same. The part performed by the apostles in this case being the same as in the case of the deacons, it is fair to presume that the part performed by the people was also the same, and that Luke fails to mention it because, having previously stated the process of selecting one class of church officers, he could presume that his readers would understand that the same process was observed in the present instance. Indeed, the nature of the case is such that we would of necessity so understand it, unless expressly informed that the process was different.[7]

Third, his conclusion on Titus is stated:

> When Titus is told to ordain or appoint Elders in every city, the same term is used, as when the apostles in Jerusalem proposed to appoint the deacons: the process, therefore, is the same, and it takes place after the selection of the officers by the people."[8]

Implications for Member Selection & Leadership Appointment

Members should be taught well about the functions of elders, qualifications of elders, and the responsibilities of members to the elders. Without adequate understanding, the process could easily turn into a popularity contest. The process of selecting and appointing elders should ideally be preceded by thirty to forty years of teaching and training men to be elders, shepherds, bishops. Two weeks before the time for appointment, it is too late to be concerned about who is qualified to be an elder. There should be a base of wisdom and maturity started from youth.

I believe every congregation has the leaders it wants, the leaders it deserves, the leaders it has trained, and the leaders it has prayed for. If the leaders are less than adequate, the congregation should evaluate its prayers, training, teaching, and expectations. May God bless us to follow His teaching in developing, selecting, appointing, and encouraging good leaders.

Other Matters of Procedure & Process

Whatever process of elder selection a congregation uses, it is my suggestion that the plan be studied, decided, written, distributed to all the members, and followed for this specific time. After the selection has been made, it is good to evaluate and make adjustments for the next selection. It should be clear who will be involved in the selection, what the timetable will be for each stage of the process, and how objections and concerns will be addressed.

One helpful guideline I have seen is that multiple suggestions for a man to serve as an elder must be submitted before the person will be considered. Depending on the size of the congregation, a man's name should be submitted five to ten times before he will be considered. This attempts to eliminate many of the men who are suggested only because of family or friendship connections, but who are not qualified.

I do not like the stipulation requiring you to contact the man before you submit his name to be considered. When we were selecting elders in my younger days, I would sometimes mention it to a man I thought would be a good shepherd. He might reply, "I can't serve because I don't have the desire." I would then forget about him because he didn't desire the work.

As I read about great men that God has used as leaders, I find many were reluctant leaders. Moses didn't like the idea of leaving his work as a shepherd, facing Pharaoh, and telling him God wanted his people to leave Egypt. He had many objections, and he didn't have the desire at the time. But with God's presence and help, he became a great leader.

Gideon didn't see himself as a leader. When the angel of the Lord approached him, he didn't feel qualified or have the desire. When he was nominated as a leader, he replied "Please, Lord, how can I save Israel? Behold, my clan is the weakest in Manasseh, and I am the least in my father's house" (Judg. 6:15).

Now, when I am talking with a man who appears to me to have the qualities of character, compassion, and conduct to be a shepherd of God's people, and he says, "I couldn't because I don't have the desire," I don't quit. I reply, "Maybe you should cultivate the desire. It may be God has prepared you to do something you haven't considered, something you fear, or something coming later you can do. Think about it. Pray about it. Consider it." When multiple people have suggested a man, maybe through several selection processes, he might realize others see in him an opportunity and obligation he hasn't seriously considered.

One guideline I strongly encourage in your selection process is having a week of dead time between time for objections and the day elders are appointed. Years ago, we were appointing additional leadership and there was a two-week time for questions and objections. On Saturday night before a man was to be ordained as an elder the next morning, the elders received an objection. They asked me to accompany them to this man's house to discuss it with him. As we approached his house, there were many cars in his driveway. His father, mother, siblings, and their spouses and children had come to spend the night with him and see him appointed as an elder the next day. When he was presented with the objections, he was very calm and agreed that the objections were probably accurate, and he needed to grow more to serve in that capacity. He said, "I will remove my name from consideration." His attitude was great, and he is still a faithful Christian. However, it would have taken stress off the elders and eliminated the embarrassment of going back into his house and announcing to his family that he would not be an elder if there had been a week to work on the objections instead of only 24 hours.

I would also suggest that a potential elder's wife should be interviewed alone. I know several men who seemed to be qualified and ready to serve, but their wives had no desire to be the wife of an elder. Sometimes a wife will reveal to the selection group something that gives insight to a man's qualifications or lack of shepherding qualities that she might be unwilling or afraid to say in front of her husband.

Likewise, interviews with the children of a prospective elder will give more information about his leadership qualities. The leadership evidence required by the Holy Spirit is demonstrated leadership in the home. The bishop "must manage his own household well, with all dignity keeping his children submissive, for if someone does not know how to manage his own household, how will he care for God's church?" (1 Tim. 3:4-5). Are we aware that what is seen in public and what goes on in private are sometimes different? When family members of a potential elder are asked about his qualities as a husband and father, their answers will either enhance or diminish his public perception.

Sometimes elders have to (or decide to) step down from serving. The best time to talk about how an elder is going to leave his service is before he is ever appointed. One of the most devastating things an elder can do is to get frustrated and resign in anger or discouragement without notifying fellow elders and making arrangements for a smooth transition. I suggest leaders who are being appointed make a "no-suicide contract." They agree to communicate to the leadership team at least (when possible) three months ahead if they will be moving or resigning. This provides opportunities to make adjustments to cover their responsibilities and to give adequate time for saying goodbye. If there are any irritations remaining, they can be settled, and appreciation can be expressed for the work the leader has done. This notification shows love and respect for the leadership team and the congregation. In contrast, Jesus said a man who runs in time of trouble is not a shepherd but a hired hand. "He flees because he is a hired hand and cares nothing for the sheep" (John 10:13).

It can be helpful soon after men are selected and appointed to have a time of orientation for the new elders and their wives. This can be a time of getting to know the present elders, learning how they work together, rehearsing biblical responsibilities for God's leaders, and getting training on how to be effective shepherds of God's flock.

In January 2015, I started a new website and blog "for elders in the church, men who want to be elders, and everyone who loves and appreciates elders." I post the first and third Tuesday of each month and make a book recommendation each fifth Tuesday. You can get information here: www.newshepherdsorientation.com. I also do a limited number of New Shepherd Orientation Workshops to train and encourage new and existing elders. You can contact me through my website or by email: jerrie@barberclippings.com. If you would like a copy of the best process I have seen for selecting elders, email me the request, and I will send it to you.

May God bless us as we access his promised wisdom in selecting and ordaining spiritual men who will shepherd and lead God's people to increasing maturity in his service.

Notes

1. J. P. Louw and E. A. Nida, *Greek-English Lexicon of the New Testament: Based on Semantic Domains* (electronic ed. of the 2nd edition.) (New York: United Bible Societies, 1996).
2. Ibid.
3. Ibid.
4. Ibid.
5. Ibid.
6. J.W. McGarvey, *A Treatise on the Eldership*, Kindle Edition (DeWard), Kindle Locations 833-837.
7. Ibid (Kindle Locations 839-845).
8. Ibid (Kindle Locations 849-850).

9

THE WIFE OF AN ELDER

Janace Scott

What a privilege and honor to be the wife of an elder! And at the same time, I can also say what a sober and humbling experience it is to be the wife an elder. When asked to write this segment of the book, I wondered where to begin. My mind was in a whirl. After all, the Bible does not tell us what the role of an elder's wife is. It is, however, full of instructions and advice specifically for women and specifically for wives.

When I was growing up, I remember that in our Bible classes we were taught the Bible stories and their applications. We learned about the way we should live and conduct ourselves, as well as the consequences of our actions and the effect our actions had on others. As we grew older, the young men were encouraged to think about becoming preachers and leaders in the church. As young girls, we were encouraged to become Bible class teachers and good homemakers. We were also taught the importance of helping others and being kind-hearted. That was all good advice. At the time, that teaching did not translate into preparing us for the possibility that we could be the wife of an elder some day; however, as I look back, I can see that was exactly what it was.

I would venture to say that most young girls do not give much thought to the fact that they one day may be an elder's wife. That is a concept that is too far into the future for them. There may be exceptions to this, but I know I never once had a conversation with my friends about what our responsibilities would be if we married someone who later became an elder. Even when we were in college, that possibility was still too far into the future. Our thoughts centered on getting our education and finding a good person to marry, making a home, and having children.

Then as we got older and were wives taking care of children, our life was busy and filled with thoughts of bringing up our children, teaching them to know God, keeping them clothed and fed, making sure they were healthy, and the hundreds of other things parents deal with as they rear their children. At the same time, many of us were also teaching Bible classes, maybe working part-time, and keeping our home life on an even keel.

As it happens with families, time passed quickly, and before we knew it, our children were dating, and then marrying and having children of their own. We were grandparents, and that "far-off future" had arrived.

If the time comes that our husband is asked to serve as an elder, we may ask, "What are we supposed to do?" Certainly, by the time our husband becomes an elder, we have a pretty clear idea of what is involved for us. We have observed others through the years and have formed opinions about the qualities we need to possess so that we can give our husbands the support he needs as he serves the congregation. In the back of our minds, we also consider that we are now being observed and are serving as examples for others.

What exactly is the role of an elder's wife? It is not a role of authority, but one of support, encouragement, and help to her husband as he serves. By definition, the word elder means older, and it relates to the age and maturity of the man. It would follow that elders' wives are among the older and more mature women of the congregation. They are not necessarily the oldest women of the congregation, but they have experienced many life lessons during the years they were establishing a home with their husband and rearing their children. While they surely did not do everything perfectly, they most certainly learned valuable lessons along the way.

Paul wrote a letter to Titus and gave him instructions to give to the people in the churches on the island of Crete. It is here that he gives instructions to the older women in the church. In Tit. 2:3-5, we read, "Older women likewise are to be reverent in behavior, not slanderers or slaves to much wine. They are to teach what is good, and so train the young women to love their husbands and children, to be self-controlled, pure, working at home, kind, and submissive to their own husbands, that the word of God may not be reviled." These instructions are for older women, and they would definitely apply to an elder's wife. We can conclude that the wife of an elder is to be reverent in her behavior, not slanderers, not slaves to drink, and teachers of what is good.

There are two positives and two negatives in these instructions. First of all, older women are instructed to be reverent or holy in behavior. How do you describe someone who is reverent in behavior? You can probably think of a person you know or have known who exhibits this kind of behavior—someone who could be described as gracious, who speaks kindly, who is pleasant to be around, and who honors God with her life.

How do we develop that kind of behavior? Behavior actually starts with our mind. We read in Prov. 23:7, "For as he thinks in his heart, so is he" (NKJV). Paul gives us instructions about filling our minds with goodness in his letter to the Philippians, "Finally, brethren, whatever things are true, whatever things are noble, whatever things are just, whatever things are pure, whatever things are lovely, whatever things are of good report, if there is any virtue and if there is anything praiseworthy—meditate on these things" (4:8).

The things that fill our mind are made known in our words and actions, so it is important that our thoughts are true, honorable, just, pure, lovely, and gracious. We are to think of things that are excellent and worthy of praise. The movies and television shows we watch will influence us. The books and magazines we read will influence us. We must be careful to fill our mind with things pleasing to God. Reading and studying God's Word will help us to think on what is good and pure. Every time we stop and look at God's great creation, we realize he is all-powerful, sovereign, just, faithful and good, and we will rejoice that he is in control. When we think on these things, our perspective is right. If we train our minds to think on good things, then our behavior, with God's help, will be good.

Next, Paul tells Titus that older women are not to be slanderers. If we are known to gossip and slander others, how can we as older women expect to have the influence necessary to teach the younger women? Reverent behavior and slander certainly do not go together! We are told in Luke 6:45, "The good person out of the good treasure of his heart produces good, and the evil person out of his evil treasure produces evil, for out of the abundance of the heart his mouth speaks." If we fill our minds with things that are good and pure, our speech, like our behavior, will be a reflection of those good things.

James tells us in his letter that "no human being can tame the tongue" (Jas. 3:8). Therefore, we must be constantly on guard and watch our words. Not only must we be careful of the words we say, we should also watch the tone of our words. We have heard the saying, "Think before you speak." That is not just practical advice, it is also biblical teaching as we read in James that we are to "be slow to speak" (1:19).

The third point Paul makes to Titus is that we are not to be slaves to drink. We all know the consequences of becoming enslaved to alcohol. How many lives and families have been damaged because of alcohol addiction? We may never be enslaved to alcohol, but we need to also watch that we don't become enslaved to other things that can cause problems in our lives in a similar manner. Many women become "shopaholics" and buy too many things they don't need because they fail to control their spending. They often find out their spending does not make them happy, and their families may suffer. Some may let their hobbies come between them and their families. Others may let their work outside the home become the focus of their life. The point is that God wants us to put God and our service to him first in our lives.

Finally, Paul tells Titus that the older women are to teach what is good and train the younger women to love their husbands, to love their children, to be sensible, to be chaste, to be good managers of the household, to be kind, and to be submissive to their husbands. Then we are given the reason why this instruction is given—"that the word of God may not be reviled" (Tit. 2:5).

As older women, we all have a job to do, and we are all older women to someone! It seems the world has taken control of what we in the church should be doing. It really matters what we focus our minds on and how we live. The younger women should learn from us and not from movies and television. What our younger women learn from us—whether from our teaching or our example—is important.

What kind of person is an elder's wife? What is she like? Since no two persons are alike, each woman who is the wife of an elder will be unique. She will be different from every other elder's wife you meet. Each one will have her own talents, her own personality traits, and her own strengths, as well as her own weaknesses. She will have good points, and she will also have qualities that could use improvement. There are, however, some qualities that every elder's wife should have.

An elder's wife should be a faithful Christian. She should have the qualities that every Christian should have. She should be kind and thoughtful. She should have a servant's attitude and be willing to help others. She should be an example to others and have the respect of the congregation. If this is not true, her husband's name might not even be submitted as a candidate for elder. It is sad but true that there are some good men who have never been asked to serve as an elder because their wives are not faithful or they are known to be gossips or troublemakers.

She should try her best to live a life that would be pleasing to God. Jesus taught that we all should be the salt of the earth and the light of the world (Matt. 5:13-14). As such, we can make a difference in our little corner of the world.

Like all Christians, she should never stop growing spiritually. Regular study of God's Word is essential for her spiritual growth, as well as obedience to his will. Everyone will be at different stages in her spiritual maturity, but the important thing is that each is continually growing and maturing in her faith.

Besides regular study of God's Word, it is also helpful for her to read good books written by mature Christian women who have been "through the fire" and can offer helpful advice. In addition, she can look around at the people she knows and find the ones who are good examples for her to follow. She doesn't have to follow them in all things because no one is perfect, but she can imitate them in the things that are in accordance with God's will. In his letter to the Philippians, Paul tells the church in 3:17, "Brothers, join in imitating me, and keep your eyes on those who walk according to the example you have in us." In the verses just before this, Paul had told them he was not perfect. And in his first letter to the Corinthians, Paul says, "Be imitators of me, as I am of Christ" (11:1). We all can learn so much from people who are striving to be faithful.

Because of the responsibilities of her husband, she also will have special responsibilities. One of the qualifications of an elder is that he is to be the husband of one wife (1 Tim. 3:2; Tit. 1:6). The role of a wife is defined in Genesis. God created the heavens and the earth.

After He created each element of the creation, God saw that it was good. Genesis 1:31 reads, "God saw everything that he had made, and behold, it was very good." But in 2:18, we read, "It is not good that the man should be alone; I will make him a helper fit for him."

Man needed a mate that would be a helper suitable for him, and God made Eve. Eve was made to be a companion for Adam, as well as a helper suited for him. They worked together as a team. Working together as a team is necessary for all marriages, and it is also necessary for an elder and his wife. The elder's wife should be the kind of wife that God wants every wife to be. She is to be a companion to him and love him and put him first in her life after God. She should have respect for him and his decisions, and she should appreciate the responsibilities he has and the work he does.

Peter gives instructions to wives in 1 Pet. 3:3. He says, "Do not let your adorning be external—the braiding of hair and the putting on of gold jewelry, or the clothing you wear." A gentle and quiet spirit is a quality that should be desired by all wives; however, I fear this attitude is not looked upon as something to be desired in the world, or even sometimes in the church. But just look at what God thinks about this quality of women! The Bible tells us it is very precious in His sight. We all should want the quality of a gentle and quiet spirit.

In Prov. 31, we find a description of a truly good wife. We read in v. 11, "The heart of her husband trusts in her." An elder should be able to confide in his wife and trust that she will keep his confidences. She should also be careful not to talk about any business of the church that she knows about until it is publicly announced. The reason James has a lot to say about controlling the tongue is because the tongue can do great damage.

Proverbs 31:12 says, "She does him good, and not harm, all the days of her life." This is something for which all wives should strive. Knowing he can trust his wife to do him good and not harm will help a man be comfortable in his work as an elder.

Another important way an elder's wife can help her husband is to encourage him and support him in his responsibilities. There will be meetings he has to attend that will take time away from home, and she should exhibit a good attitude about this. He will spend time preparing lessons if he teaches. He will visit the sick. This is her time to be patient and not resent his time away when he is helping others. Supporting him in his work will make his load seem lighter.

At times, he may ask his wife to go with him as he makes visits at the hospital or in the homes of others. It may be that the presence of his wife will allow the person visited to be more relaxed. This is also a good work of an elder's wife.

One of the qualities of an elder is that he is to be hospitable. This will surely require the support and help of his wife. Her role as hostess is important as their home should be open for others. This is not only helpful and needed, but it will also be appreciated by her husband.

Another quality of an elder is that he not be greedy for gain, and likewise his wife should not be greedy for gain. An elder's wife—or any wife for that matter—should not press her husband for material things they cannot afford and place pressure on him to try to obtain those things.

Leaders of the church are also referred to as shepherds. The people of the first century were very familiar with the responsibilities of a shepherd. A shepherd took care of and protected the sheep. In the church, the shepherds are concerned for the people, and they are charged with taking care of the people, seeing that they are given spiritual food, and protecting them from dangers of false teaching. In this context, a shepherd's wife is one who will also be concerned for people when they are hurting or need help in some way. She will be quick to help others when she sees the need.

My challenge to young women would be that they look to the future and consider that they may be the wife of an elder some day.

To that end, they should continue on the path they have begun as a Christian. They should live in such a way that their husband won't be rejected because of their life and their actions. Husbands and wives should encourage and support each other in their spiritual growth, while making their home and rearing their children.

If there are still children in their home, it should go without saying that an elder's wife is to be very much involved in the teaching and rearing of their children "in the discipline and instruction of the Lord" (Eph. 6:4). Women have such an influence on their children, and that is a great responsibility. They can instill in them the idea that they can someday be servant leaders. They can show their children what it means to help others in need by taking them along when they take food to the sick or clothes to people in need. If they teach a Bible class, they can encourage their children to help them in some small way as they prepare their lessons. As they help, let them know that they are helping so others can learn about Jesus.

My challenge to older women is to set a good example for the younger women and be willing to teach them in a kind and loving way some of the things they have learned along the way. None of us will ever be perfect, but we are to keep learning and growing in this journey we are on so that we will one day live with God. The points made here are not just check points, but they are principles whereby we can shape our lives. A study of Prov. 31:10-31 gives us many principles that will guide us as we strive to be pleasing to God and a helper fit for our husband.

Most successful people don't go through life in a haphazard way. They make plans and have goals for their family, their children's education, as well as their retirement. In the same way, the Christian life should be lived in a purposeful way. Our spiritual life is too important to be a hit or miss thing. We need to put study, thought, and planning in an effort to improve our lives every day that we live. We should have goals and work on achieving them. We will never be perfect, but we can never give up.

Being the wife of an elder and supporting him is one way to serve so that he can fulfill his duties, and God's people can become a good and lasting influence in the community, our nation, and even in the world. It is a high and humble calling for a man to be selected as an elder/shepherd, and the role of his wife is to encourage him when he needs it, to support him in his responsibilities, and to be a servant beside him as he serves. At the same time, she should be an example to others as she lives the Christian life to the best of her ability.

10

THE HONOR OF SERVING AS AN ELDER

Ron McElyea

Anytime I am asked to give my thoughts on any subject regarding our Lord and his church, I am both honored and humbled by the request. To study the honor of serving as an elder, we must first understand the meaning of the words *honor* and *serving*. The word *honor* has several definitions and synonyms. Since it is used as a noun in the above heading, it can mean "public esteem, personal recognition, merited respect, or a being of superior worth." These various definitions emphasize a person's human rank or status. From my vantage point, none of them fit the idea of honor that applies to serving as an elder. However, one definition of honor does fit the service of an elder: *privilege*. Privilege is understood to be a favor that is gifted (e.g. "a special privilege," "a granted favor"). Serving as an elder in the Lord's church certainly is an honor in the sense that it a gifted privilege to be entrusted with the task of shepherding the Lord's church.

We should also consider the meaning of the word *serving* as it applies to this study—"to be a servant, to wait on others, or to attend to the needs of others" all equally apply to physical acts. Furthermore, being a serving person carries with it the fundamental idea of being "less than" vs. "greater than." It suggests a person has a lower position on the chain of hierarchy. The idea of service strongly implies that a person cannot be passive in his action, but rather must be actively engaged in work. When someone is serving, he is performing deeds for the benefit of others, and that can be very difficult. Most of us desire to be on the "served end" rather than the "serving end." We would rather be the one honored instead of the one giving honor.

When we closely consider the meanings of these words as they apply to the position of an elder, we can determine that the honor of serving as an elder in the Lord's church should be viewed in the following light: "It is a special privilege and a gracious favor to serve and value others as better than yourself." Paul describes it this way: "Do nothing from selfish ambition or conceit, but in humility count others more significant than yourselves" (Phil. 2:3). Serving as an elder in the Lord's body is both a remarkable and humble honor when we consider the role of an elder through these words.

I am making an assumption, but I believe most men appointed to serve as elders do not and have never felt "qualified" to serve in this role—at least most of the ones I've known and currently have the blessing of working with see it this way. In fact, most of us readily acknowledge that we didn't fully comprehend the magnitude of this "noble" task when we first accepted it. Most men have no concept of the energy, time, or involvement necessary to serve acceptably in this God-designed role.

Thankfully, both God and most congregations patiently allow us to grow and mature as we strive to understand what the Lord expects from us as an elder. Whether or not we like to admit it, many problems in the body come from decisions (or the lack of decisions) elders make. I'm thankful for the forgiveness and love of God and that our "sins, which are many, are forgiven" (Luke 7:47). What makes Christianity different from all other religions is that love is the most revealed characteristic of the Godhead. I awaken each morning absolutely amazed by the love Jesus has for us and astounded by his enduring patience.

As elders, we serve Jesus' church, and I remain in awe of that responsibility. To serve effectively, I must keep my perspective as to who I am in relation to Jesus. After all, he is the chief Shepherd, which makes me a sub-shepherd. He has all authority; not me. He is the one I must imitate. I am only worthy of being imitated if I am imitating him (1 Cor. 11:1). To keep myself continually aware of this, I mentally use the acronym: F.A.S.T.

This has nothing to do with speed or quickness. In my acronym, "F" stands for *faithful*. To be a faithful elder, I must first be counted as a Christian who has waved the flag of surrender. "A" stands for *accountable*. To be an accountable elder, I must be a Christian who has submitted my will to God's. "S" stands for *selfless*. To be a selfless elder, I must be a Christian who has been willing to sacrifice what my flesh has determined is most important. "T" stands for *trustworthy*. To be a trustworthy elder, I must be a Christian who understands all aspects of being a good steward.

When I consider the word *fast* as a whole, I relate it to "holding fast or standing fast" in the Word, sound doctrine, that which is good, and the Spirit—just as Paul stated in his letters. Being faithful, accountable, selfless, and trustworthy are godly traits to be acted out in our everyday lives. They cannot only be hidden away within our hearts or minds. They are traits that must always be observed and demonstrated. These characteristics keep me focused on who it is I really honor in my service to the church. While the acronym FAST helps me as an elder, these traits apply to all Christians as we struggle to submit our lives completely to Jesus.

In the New Testament, the Son honored his Father with complete surrender, submission, sacrifice, and stewardship. Jesus abandoned the glory of heaven to become a servant. For that, he alone is due all praise and honor by every Christian. Jesus magnifies these traits, and if I want to be more like him, I must continually exhibit these qualities as a sub-shepherd in his church. I owe all honor to the Lord of lords and King of kings.

Surrender is a word typically used in the negative sense by most cultures. A nation surrenders to another and becomes subservient to the conqueror. To make a living in our culture, we surrender our time to another, even though we normally would rather do something else with that time. As Christians, we are asked to surrender much more than just our time or our allegiance to a nation; we are expected to surrender our entire lives to God as we set an example of surrender by faith (2 Cor. 5:7).

As an elder, I must surrender by being faithful to Christ, or I will be lost. Staying faithful is difficult when you see so much godlessness and worldliness, even in the church. As Christ's sub-shepherd, I see the hurt and pain sin causes in the lives of so many Christians. I witness firsthand the struggles of those I care for as I see them contending on a regular basis with the temptations Satan uses to destroy their faithfulness. I've seen and suffered with wonderful Christians who are dealing with the destruction of the flesh caused by sickness and disease while trying to offer comfort and peace. I know of very few faithful Christians who aren't suffering in some way to stay obedient and to be better examples of what it means to be faithful. I've looked to the Bible to give instruction and guidance to others with the best of intentions, and I regret when I fail in my attempt to encourage them.

In faithfulness, I press on toward the goal of keeping the faith. I understand more than ever what the writer James meant when he stated, "Count it all joy, my brothers, when you meet trials of various kinds, for you know that the testing of your faith produces steadfastness" (Jas. 1:2-3). I must surrender my will to his will by being faithful. I constantly recall Paul's inspired words, "I can do all things through him who strengthens me" (Phil. 4:13). I must be an example of faithfulness if I really want to honor and please him.

This admonition is to me as well as to Timothy, "if we are faithless, he remains faithful—for he cannot deny himself" (2 Tim. 3:13). These words remind me that I can be faithful because of Jesus, who reveals perfect faithfulness. He is my helper, and he will never leave or forsake me (Heb. 13:5-6). As long as I remain in submission to his will, I will be counted as a faithful servant.

Submission is putting my will under another's will. It is my choice to be held accountable to someone else's measuring stick. The honor of serving as an elder is always knowing that if I submit to Christ, he will evaluate me, or hold me accountable, with greater mercy and kindness than I will ever deserve. Of course, that doesn't mean I will be treated without justice and judgment. Jesus' statement—"Whoever does not bear his own cross and come after me cannot be my disciple" (Luke 14:27)—forces me to contemplate what it really means to be his servant. As an elder, there is no room for my own agenda or my own personal desires in my service to Christ and his church. He holds me accountable to bear fruit. That thought is scary, but it is also one that is full of hope. If I'm going to submit to Jesus, it must be on his terms—I must be willing to submit to his fair evaluation and be accountable to him.

The parable of the talents depicts this as well as any other Scripture. The master provides money to three servants, each one according to his ability. The parable reveals that each servant understood he was supposed to invest the money wisely and to provide an increase for their master. The story does not end well for the servant who was given the least amount to invest. While all the servants knew that they were going to be held accountable, the one given the least did not even make an attempt to invest. He was held accountable by his master (Matt. 25:14-30).

As an elder, I must realize my service is not about my authority, but my accountability. My submission to Christ signifies my willingness to be accountable. I often hear preachers say, "My employer is the

Lord." May that always be true! No one in the church—no elder, no deacon, no preacher, and no member—will hold any other Christian servant more accountable than the Lord himself. With the gravity of this responsibility in mind, we should also remember that our merciful Father will look at us through the blood of his Son when evaluating us and holding us accountable.

Most of us don't think about sacrifice the way God wants us to. Over the years, my concepts of selflessness and sacrifice have changed dramatically. I used to think Christian sacrifice focused mainly on material possessions. Indeed, giving of one's means is commanded. Doing good to all, especially to the household of believers, is a primary aspect of being a Christian. However, just because we give does not mean we have sacrificed. The honor of serving as a sub-shepherd carries with it the responsibility of sacrificing whatever necessary to benefit and protect the flock. I know God wants me to die to self, but I still don't fully comprehend what it means to be truly selfless. I know one of my personal battles is to deny myself. To do away with selfishness, I must accept my need to rely more on God for my very sustenance and wellbeing.

So what does God see as an acceptable sacrifice? What will he acknowledge as being selfless? As an elder, I have learned that one of the greatest possessions I must sacrifice is my time. It's amazing how we take time for granted. I see time entirely different today than I did a few years ago since I have less ahead of me now than I did then. Although I am a sheep in the flock, I have also been given a unique privilege in the kingdom as a caretaker of that flock. I'm available to my brethren anytime, day or night. My time is the flock's time. I don't have all the answers, but I know who to ask. I can't always solve every problem, but I know which book to grab from the shelf to guide me to the solution. I do my best to spend more of my time in Bible study, teaching, counseling, and healing spiritual wounds, etc. to be ready to care for the flock.

I appreciate so much more the sacrifice of God as I strive to be selfless and give even more than I thought I could. After all, how can I compare my selflessness to God? It's not even possible. My continued goal is to measure today's sacrifices by considering what I didn't do so well yesterday. Like Paul, I am "forgetting what lies behind and straining forward to what lies ahead" (Phil. 3:13). I can do better and do more because God's grace is sufficient. Knowing that all blessings are truly from God has allowed me to see clearly what I've been entrusted with. If I am his steward, then I must be willing to stay the course and be counted trustworthy by him.

I accepted the responsibility of being a steward for Jesus when I obeyed his gospel. He is the master, and I'm his servant. When we think of stewardship, we often think of physical possessions. However, being God's steward involves much more. I must be a steward of Scripture, being able to manage it and divide it rightly. I must be a steward of my time, being able to manage it so that I complete his priorities before considering my own. I must be a good steward of my money to be able to share and help others. If God does not find me trustworthy, there is no way I can be a good steward.

In serving as a sub-shepherd, I must mimic the chief Shepherd's perfect example of stewardship. I must constantly acknowledge that the only way to be trustworthy is to serve him on his terms. I am here to do my Father's will just as Jesus did. Trustworthy Christians and trustworthy elders are entrusted as stewards of God in one common thought and one common command. That common thought is to realize that we dare not trust in ourselves (John 14:1). The common command is that we all are to be gospel stewards (Matt. 28:19-20).

In serving Christ and his church, we all have God-given responsibilities. Scripture teaches us that a church's members are no more or less important than another. Each member is gifted and entrusted with certain roles. If we use our gifts faithfully as the Holy Spirit has apportioned to us, we all will receive the same outcome—

the saving of our souls. May we recognize what an honor it is to serve our Savior who became a servant to all (Matt. 20:28). Because of him, our honor will be the hope and promise of everlasting life in the presence of God's glory. Let us all remain FAST—faithful, accountable, selfless, and trustworthy.

ABOUT THE AUTHORS

RON McELYEA has served as an elder for the Baker Heights congregation in Abilene, TX for more than 15 years. He and his wife, Jerri, have two children and four grandchildren. In 2015, he retired from insurance brokerage.

JIM FAUGHN serves as a minister and elder of the Central Church of Christ in Paducah, KY. His wife, Donna, speaks at several ladies events throughout the country. They have two children and five grandchildren. Both their son and son-in-law are preachers.

SELLERS CRAIN began his ministry in 1961; he preached for the Rivergate Church of Christ in Madison, TN for 24 years and still serves as one of the elders. He has written over 40 curriculum books for the Gospel Advocate and a 2-volume commentary on Matthew for Truth for Today.

JAY LOCKHART serves as the preacher and as an elder for the Whitehouse, TX Church of Christ. He and his wife, Arlene, have three children and six grandchildren. He has served in church work for over fifty years; he has preached in 28 states and 6 foreign countries.

About the Authors

RAY BOWMAN serves as an elder at the Holly Hill Church of Christ in Frankfort, KY. He and his wife, Stephenia, live on their farm in northern Franklin County.

STEVE BAILEY serves as the preaching minister and an elder for the Mesquite, TX Church of Christ. He and his wife, Keitha, have been married for 41 years. They have two children and two grandchildren, with another on the way!

HOWARD NORTON has been preaching since he was 16 years old. He has also served as an elder, teacher, foreign missionary to Central and South America, an administrator at two Christian universities, and an editor for *The Christian Chronicle*. He and his wife, Jane, live in Searcy, AR and have been married for 59 years. They have three children and seven grandchildren.

JERRIE BARBER has been preaching since 1961 and providing interim services to churches since 2007. He also provides consulting and training to elders, specializing in his New Shepherd Orientation workshops.

JANACE SCOTT is the wife of Royce Scott, who has served as an elder for seven years at the Oldham Lane Church of Christ in Abilene, TX. Together, they have five children and fifteen grandchildren. Janace has taught Bible classes for all ages and has also been published in *Christian Bible Teacher* and *Think*.

GREGG WOODALL serves as an elder for the Karns Church of Christ in Knoxville, TN. He and his wife, Sherrye, have four children and five grandchildren. He works as a CPA.

www.ingramcontent.com/pod-product-compliance
Lightning Source LLC
Chambersburg PA
CBHW071527080526
44588CB00011B/1580